SATs Made Simple

English

Ages 9–10

Year 5

KS2

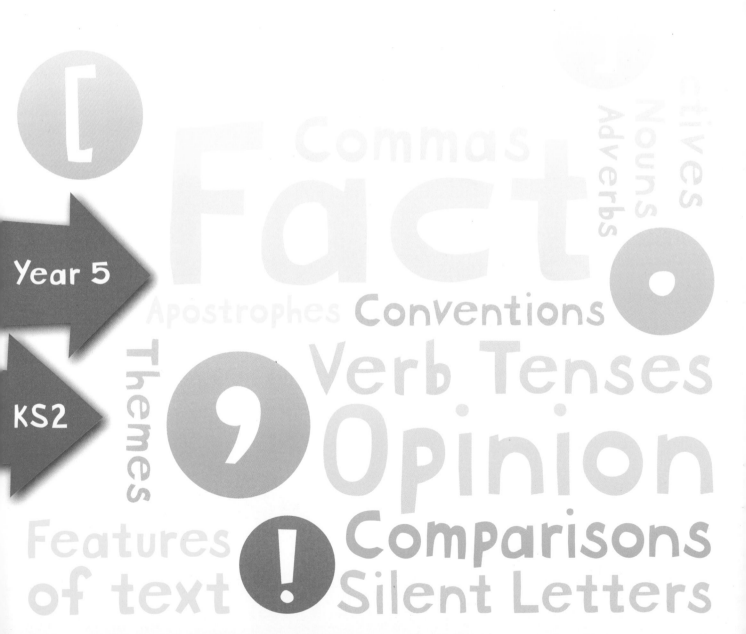

SCHOLASTIC

Published in the UK by Scholastic, 2016

Scholastic Distribution Centre, Bosworth Avenue, Tournament
Fields, Warwick, CV34 6UQ

Scholastic Ireland, 89E Lagan Road, Dublin Industrial Estate,
Glasnevin, Dublin, D11 HP5F

www.scholastic.co.uk

SCHOLASTIC and associated logos are trademarks and/or
registered trademarks of Scholastic Inc.
© Scholastic, 2016
3 4 5 6 7 8 9   2 3 4 5 6 7 8 9 0 1

A CIP catalogue record for this book is available from
the British Library.

ISBN 978-1407-18335-0
Printed and bound in India by Replika Press Pvt. Ltd.

The book is made of materials from well-managed,
FSC-certified forests and other controlled sources.

Due to the nature of the web we cannot guarantee the content or
links of any site mentioned.

We strongly recommend that teachers check websites before
using them in the classroom.

Every effort has been made to trace copyright holders for the
works reproduced in this book, and the Publishers apologise for
any inadvertent omissions.

Author

Lesley and Graham Fletcher

Editorial team

Rachel Morgan, Tracey Cowell, Rebecca Rothwell, Jane Jackson
and Sally Rigg

Design team

Nicolle Thomas and Neil Salt

Illustration

Judy Brown

Contents

Spelling

Reading

How to use

National Curriculum Tests are taken by children at the end of Key Stage 2 (11 years old). Children will take tests in Grammar, Punctuation and Spelling, and Reading.

• These books are written by teachers for the National Curriculum to help children prepare for end-of-year school tests in Grammar, Punctuation and Spelling, and Reading.

• Each book is split into five sections, which match the content to be covered by the tests.

• Practising for the tests will help children feel prepared and prevent them from worrying about the unknown.

• Use the books to practise skills 'little and often'. Don't attempt to do too much in one session.

• At the back of the book is a **Planner** to enable you to record what content has been covered and to prioritise what still needs to be done.

• Year 3, 4 and 5 tests are not compulsory but SATs Made Simple will help children preparing for assessments and tests in school.

• A series of **Practice Tests** is available to help children towards the next stage of their preparations for National and school tests.

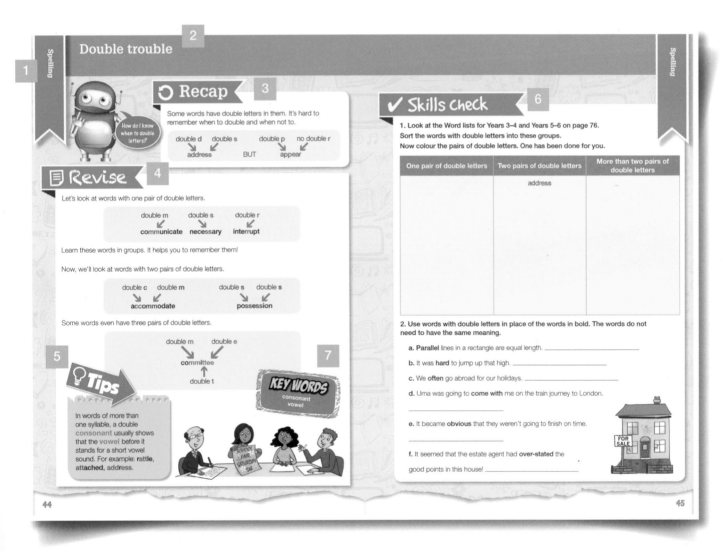

1 Chapter title

2 Topic title

3 Each page starts a **recap** with a 'What is...' question which gives children a clear definition for the terminology used.

4 In the **revise** section there are clear teaching examples, using fun characters and clear illustrations.

5 **Tips** are included to help show important points to remember and to give helpful strategies for remembering.

6 The **skills check** sections enable children to practise what they have learned using National Test-style questions.

7 **Key words** that children need to know are displayed. Definitions for these words can be found in the **Glossary**.

Adjectives

What is an adjective?

↺ Recap

An **adjective** describes a characteristic of a noun.

the **blue** hat

The word **blue** is an adjective.

📄 Revise

Adjectives describe or modify nouns. They give us more detail.

the **enormous** elephant

The word **enormous** tells us more about the elephant.

the **blue** elephant

The word **blue** tells us about a very different elephant!

It was an **unbelievable** story!

Not all adjectives describe characteristics we can see.

It was an **enthralling** story!

KEY WORDS

adjectives

Adjectives often come before a noun. You can have more than one adjective to describe a noun.

✔ Skills Check

1. **Underline the adjectives.**

   a. They could hear the plane's supersonic engine.

   b. He filled in the necessary paperwork, before applying for a passport.

   c. She had a look of intense concentration on her face.

2. **Replace the word 'good' in the sentences on the right with a more interesting adjective. Write the new sentence.**

a. It was a very **good** meal.

_____

b. Nikita had **good** results in her tests.

_____

_____

c. Their family had a **good** holiday in Majorca.

_____

_____

Nouns

↻ Recap

What is a noun?

A **noun** is a word for a person, place or thing. A noun is a naming word.

KEY WORDS

nouns (common, proper)
noun phrases

🗐 Revise

There are different types of noun: **common nouns** and **proper nouns**.

Common nouns

cat

house

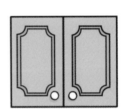

cupboard

Proper nouns

Names of people		
Jack	Sunita	Mrs Grey

Names of places		
London	France	River Tyne

Names of days of the week and months		
Wednesday	Monday	January

💡 Tips

1. All proper nouns must start with a capital letter.

2. Adjectives + **nouns** make a **noun phrase**:

> quiet **Sunday**
> young **William**
> cheerful **Mrs Grey**

You can use more than one adjective:

> a **hot windy** day
> a **large aggressive** dog
> a **long arduous** task

✔ Skills Check

1. Underline the nouns in these sentences.

a. Ellie cautiously opened the dark cupboard.

b. The American group finally reached the top of Mount Everest.

2. Put two adjectives in front of each noun to make noun phrases.

a. _____ _____ afternoon

b. _____ _____ river

c. _____ _____ crocodile

Verbs: tenses

↻ Recap

A **verb** tells you what is happening in a sentence. It is a doing word or being word.

The **tense** of a verb tells us when it happens: in the **present**, the **past** or the **future**.

What is a verb?

What is a tense?

Revise

Action verbs ➡ I run   I read

Simple present tense	Simple past tense
I run	I ran
he runs	she ran
we run ↖	↗ we ran

Use simple present or past for an action happening now (present) or an action that has already happened (past).

Being verbs ➡ I am   I have

Present progressive tense	Past progressive tense
I **am** running	I **was** running
↖	↗

Use a **helper verb** (to be or to have) to show the action is/was continuous.

Present perfect	**Past perfect**
has/have + verb	had + verb
He **has read** a book.	He **had read** the book.
↑	↑
action more recently in the past	action further in the past

✔ Skills check

KEY WORDS
verbs
tense (past, present)
progressive
future
perfect

1. Underline the verbs in this sentence.

The dog was barking loudly when the postman brought a letter.

2. Fill in the missing verbs in the table below.

Present tense	Past tense	Present progressive
he eats		
	they slept	
		we are running

3. Complete the sentence using the verb 'to finish' in the past perfect form.

They _____ _____ their tea when the phone rang.

Verbs: tense consistency and Standard English

↻ Recap

What is tense consistency?

Tense consistency means having the same tense within a sentence.

What is Standard English?

Standard English is when the verb ending agrees with the thing or person doing the action. Standard English does not use slang or dialect words.

Revise

Tense consistency

Use only one tense in a sentence:

> Ahmed **won** the race and everyone **applauded**. verbs – both in past tense

Standard English

A **singular** subject (or person doing it) must have a singular form of the verb:

> Jack **reads** a book. ⟶ Jack **was reading** a book.
> one person = singular form of verb

A **plural** subject (or things doing it) must have a plural form of the verb:

> The children **read** a book. ⟶ The children **were reading** a book.
> many people = plural form of verb

Make the verb ending agree with the number of doers!

✔ Skills Check

1. Rewrite the sentence so that the tenses are consistent.

Omar and Ranvir eats their lunch and goes out to play.

_____

2. Circle the Standard English form of the underlined verbs.

a. I **were** / **was** preparing a spicy curry for our tea.

b. George and Ahmed **is** / **are** outstanding cricketers.

c. Despite attractive adverts the property **appear** / **appears** dilapidated.

KEY WORDS

singular
plural

Modal verbs

Modal verbs go before other verbs. The modal verbs are:

can	could	would
shall	may	might
should	must	will

A modal verb expresses degrees of possibility: I **could** play football.

🗒 Revise

Modal verbs tell us how likely an action is.

1. Whether someone is able to do something:

> Ellie **can** read in assembly.

2. How likely something is:

> He **must** walk the dog, after tea.

They express degrees of certainty.
Must is more certain than **could**. **May** is less certain than **will**.

✔ Skills Check

1. Choose the best modal verb to complete each sentence.

a. _____ I go to the bathroom, please?

b. We _____ go to the cinema this afternoon.

c. They _____ be going on holiday on Saturday.

KEY WORDS
modal verbs

2. Put a tick in each row to show the type of modal verb for the underlined words in each sentence.

Sentence	Modal verb of possibility	Modal verb of certainty
Sunita <u>should</u> tidy her bedroom.		
Sunita <u>must</u> tidy her bedroom.		
Sunita <u>might</u> tidy her bedroom.		
Sunita <u>can</u> tidy her bedroom.		

Adverbs

What is an adverb?

↻ Recap

An **adverb** describes a verb. It tells us *how* something was done.

📄 Revise

Adverbs give us more detail about how a verb was done.
Adverbs often go next to the verb, but may go somewhere else in the sentence.

Jane ran. The sentence tells us she ran, but not *how* she ran.

Jane ran **slowly**.

Jane ran **swiftly**.

Jane ran **cautiously**

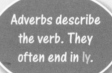

Adverbs describe the verb. They often end in ly.

These **adverbs** describe the verb **ran**.
Adverbs often end in **ly**. Each adverb changes how Jane ran.

✔ Skills Check

1. Underline the adverb in each sentence.

   a. The waves lapped gently around her feet.

   b. The music blared deafeningly from the large speakers.

   c. Aggressively, the dog guarded his territory.

2. Choose an appropriate adverb to fit in each space.

   a. The snow fell _____ during the afternoon.

   b. The sleeping baby snuffled _____.

   c. The footballer _____ tackled the opposing team.

KEY WORDS

adverbs

Adverbs and adverbials

What is an adverbial phrase?

↻ Recap

An **adverbial** phrase tells us *how, where* or *when* something happened.

📋 Revise

Be careful! Some words may be prepositions, such as back or up. Check how the word is used.

An adverbial phrase tells us:

- *how* it was done (manner) – **She walked** with great enthusiasm.
- *where* it was done (place) – **She walked** through the forest.
- *when* it was done (time) – After lunch **she went for a walk.**

Here are some examples of different types of adverb.

Adverbs of time	Adverbs of place	Adverbs of manner
soon	about	some adverbs ending **ly**, such as happily, friendly, greedily
before	indoors	fast
already	outside	hard
finally	anywhere	so
eventually	where	straight
next	towards	well
tomorrow	upstairs	
yesterday	near	
since	far	

KEY WORDS
adverbials

✔ Skills check

💡 Tips

1. **Put a circle round each adverbial phrase.**

   a. During the morning she received a telephone call.

   b. There was a fire alarm in the shopping centre.

   c. The cat curled up very gracefully.

Does a word or phrase describe *how, when* or *where* something was done? If it does, it's an adverb or adverbial phrase.

2. **Put a tick in each row to show the type of adverbial within each sentence.**

Sentence	Adverbial of time	Adverbial of place	Adverbial of manner
Thomas played the piano really beautifully.			
This afternoon we will go to the park.			
The traffic flowed over the bridge.			

Adverbs of possibility

↻ Recap

What is an adverb of possibility?

An adverb of possibility shows how certain we are about something.

The most common adverbs of possibility are:

| probably | perhaps | maybe | certainly |
| definitely | obviously | clearly | possibly |

Revise

Maybe and **perhaps** usually come at the beginning of a sentence or clause.

> **Perhaps** our visitors will arrive soon.
>
> **Maybe** we can go for a walk, if it stops raining.

Other adverbs of possibility usually come in front of the main verb.

> They **probably** will be going to France this summer.

However, they come after the verbs **am**, **is**, **are**, **was** and **were**.

> We are **definitely** going to the party.

✔ Skills Check

1. **Choose an appropriate adverb of possibility for each sentence.**

   obviously   maybe   probably

   a. Opposite sides of a rectangle are _____ equal lengths.

   b. _____ the water will be warm enough to swim in.

   c. There is _____ enough petrol in the car.

2. **Write a sentence, using an adverb of possibility.**

   _____

Fronted adverbials

What is a fronted adverbial?

↺ Recap

A **fronted adverbial** is an adverb or an adverbial phrase which is at the beginning of a sentence.

Revise

Before tea, let's go for a walk.

Adverbial phrase at the beginning of the sentence.
Adverbial of time describes *when* we will go.

Rest of sentence.

In the middle of the square, they found a restaurant.

Adverbial of place describes *where* they found it.

Fortunately, there was no more snow.

Adverb of manner, also a fronted adverbial.

Rest of sentence.

A fronted adverbial comes at the front of the sentence.
An adverbial phrase can come anywhere in the sentence.

Skills Check

KEY WORD
fronted adverbials

1. Underline the fronted adverbial in this sentence.

During the winter, the geese arrived on the coastal marshes.

2. Write a fronted adverbial to complete the sentence below.

_____ the winds blew the trees down.

Main and subordinate clauses

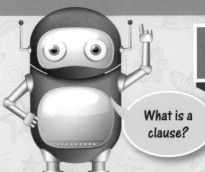

↻ Recap

What is a clause?

A **clause** is a group of words which contain a subject (a person or thing who does the verb) and verb.

Revise

There are different types of clause.
- A **main clause** is an independent clause which makes sense by itself.
- A **subordinate clause** is dependent on the main clause to make sense.

The tent blew down.

A **main clause** can be a complete sentence. It has a subject (**the tent**) and a verb (**blew**).

Clauses are often joined by a conjunction.

The tent blew down **because** it had been windy.

main clause   conjunction   subordinate clause
Tells us *why* the tent blew down.
Does not make sense by itself.

Although his father was a footballer, Oliver did not like sport.

conjunction   subordinate clause   main clause
Can come first. Does not   Does not have to come first.
make sense by itself.   Makes sense by itself.

✔ Skills Check

1. **Underline the main clause in each sentence.**

   a. Although they read all the information, the committee decided to close all the libraries.

   b. There was a flood warning because it had rained a lot.

   c. After eating the meal, James was full!

2. **Underline the subordinate clause in each sentence.**

   a. The dragon roared as he blew flames from his mouth.

   b. Despite reducing the price, the house didn't sell.

   c. School had a cake sale that did very well.

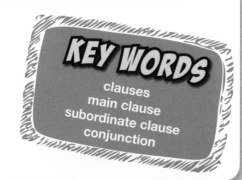

KEY WORDS

clauses
main clause
subordinate clause
conjunction

Co-ordinating conjunctions

What is a co-ordinating conjunction?

↺ Recap

A **co-ordinating conjunction** joins two clauses which would make sense on their own.

📄 Revise

An easy way to remember the co-ordinating conjunctions: the initial letters spell **fanboys**!

The co-ordinating conjunctions are:

for   **and**   **nor**   **but**   **or**   **yet**   **so**

co-ordinating conjunction
↓

The football team trained hard **but** they weren't winning any matches.
↖   ↗

Each part of the sentence makes sense by itself.

co-ordinating conjunction
↓

Josh could go to the cinema **or** he might go bowling.
↖   ↗

Each part makes sense.

KEY WORDS
co-ordinating conjunctions

✔ Skills check

1. **Choose the best conjunction for each sentence.**

   and   **or**   **but**

   a. We could have a barbecue _____ we could eat inside.

   b. The carpet is dirty _____ we can clean it.

   c. I am playing netball _____ I want to be on the team.

2. **Write an appropriate final clause for these sentences.**

   a. They went to town so _____.

   b. She stroked the goat yet _____.

   c. I love watching the swans for _____.

Subordinating conjunctions

↺ Recap

What is a subordinating conjunction?

A **subordinating conjunction** introduces a subordinate clause, which is dependent on the main clause. Subordinating conjunctions include:

because · if · when · since · before · that · then

Revise

subordinating conjunction
↓
I can't sleep **because** it's so noisy!
↑ main clause · ↗ subordinate clause

subordinating conjunction
↓
I haven't seen you **since** I saw you last week!
↑ main clause · ↗ subordinate clause

A subordinate conjunction introduces a subordinate clause.

KEY WORDS
subordinating conjunctions

✔ Skills Check

1. Use each conjunction once to join these sentences.

because · if · then

a. I wanted to go camping _____ it was sunny.

b. I ran downstairs _____ the doorbell rang.

c. The door creaked open, _____ a hand appeared.

2. Put a tick in each row, to show whether each sentence uses a co-ordinating or subordinating conjunction.

Sentence	Co-ordinating conjunction	Subordinating conjunction
I met a school friend **when** I was leaving the library.		
We went bowling **and** we went for a pizza.		
You can eat some cake **if** you are hungry.		
Would you like to play this game **or** play your new game?		

Relative clauses

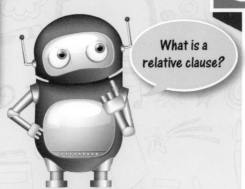

↻ Recap

A **relative clause** is a type of subordinate clause that adds information about a previous noun.
Relative clauses start with a **relative pronoun**:

> that which who whom
> whose where when

Relative pronouns introduce a relative clause and are used to start a description about a noun.

🖹 Revise

Relative clauses describe or modify a noun.

> The **dog, which was barking,** wanted to go out.

Relative clause, starts with **which**.
Describes what the **dog** was doing.
It modifies the noun.

> The **woman, who was very old,** walked with a stick.

Relative clause, starts with **who**.
Describes the **woman**. It describes the noun.

Tips 💡

The relative pronouns:
- **who**, **whom**, **whose** refer to people
- **which**, **that** refer to things
- **when** refers to time
- **where** refers to places.

✔ Skills Check

Relative clauses are usually enclosed by commas. They start with a relative pronoun.

1. Underline the relative clause in each sentence.

   a. The weather forecast, that we were listening to, told us there would be snow.

   b. The man, whose window it was, said it would need to be repaired.

   c. The pitch, where the game was to be played, was waterlogged.

2. What does the pronoun 'which' refer to in this sentence?
The sofa, which needed re-covering, was very comfortable.

_____

KEY WORDS
relative clause
relative pronouns

18

Personal and possessive pronouns

What is a pronoun?

↺ Recap

A **pronoun** replaces a noun. There are different types of pronoun. **Personal** and **possessive pronouns** are used to replace people or things.

Revise

The personal pronouns are:

| I | you | she | he | it | we | they |

Ellie went to the park and **she** went on the swings.

Ellie is replaced by the **pronoun she** in the second clause.

They are reading a book.

The **pronoun they** refers to a group of people.

KEY WORDS
pronouns
personal pronouns
possessive pronouns

There are also the possessive pronouns:

| mine | yours | hers | his | its | ours | theirs |

Jack gave me **his** stickers.

The **pronoun his** replaces **Jack**, to avoid repetition.

💡 Tips

male name → male pronoun
he   his

female name → female pronoun
she   her

neutral (not male or female)
it   its

plural names → plural pronoun /objects
they   their

✔ Skills Check

1. What does the pronoun 'it' refer to in this sentence?

The hotel borders a beautiful sandy beach and it offers great luxury.

_____.

2. Choose the best pronoun for each sentence.

| his | their | my |

a. Oscar played with _____ toy engine.

b. I couldn't wait to open _____ presents.

c. The children enjoyed _____ swim.

19

Prepositions

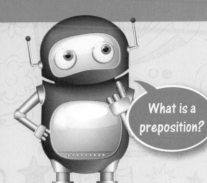

What is a preposition?

↺ Recap

A **preposition** links nouns, pronouns or a noun phrase to another word in the sentence.

📄 Revise

KEY WORDS
prepositions

Here are some common prepositions:

about	above	across	after	around	as	at	before
behind	below	beneath	beside	between	by	for	from
in	in front of	inside	into	of	off	on	onto
out of	outside	over	past	under	up	upon	with

Prepositions often tell us the position of a person or object.

The **dog** was **beside** its basket.

Preposition beside describes the position of the **dog**.

Penny was **inside** the house.

Preposition inside describes the position of **Penny**.

✔ Skills Check

Do not use a preposition at the end of a sentence.

1. Underline the prepositions in these sentences.

   a. The marathon runner was under a lot of pressure to finish.

   b. We had to queue outside the theatre to get tickets.

   c. Aisha was between Orla and Gita.

2. Write a sentence using the preposition 'beneath'.

_____

Determiners

What is a determiner?

↻ Recap

A **determiner** is used to define an object or person (a noun).

📄 Revise

Let's look at the different types of determiner.

Articles	Quantifiers	Demonstratives	Possessives
the, a, an	All numbers: one, two... Ordinals: first, second... many, some, every, any	this, those, these	my, your, our, his her, their

These are just some examples – there are others.

There were **many** ducks on **the** water and **my** gran gave me **some** bread to feed them.

↑	↑	↑	↑
quantifier	article	possessive	quantifier

Each determiner defines the noun that follows it:

> **my gran** (not anyone else's)
>
> **many ducks** (not one or a few)

You don't need to know the names of each type of determiner, though it will help to be aware of them.

✔ Skills Check

1. **Underline all the determiners in each sentence.**

   a. An icy wind blew and many people were hurrying back to their homes.

   b. Our accommodation was a disappointment and we telephoned its owner.

   c. Jane arranged lots of tables around the garden and waited for her guests to arrive.

2. **Choose the best determiner for each sentence.**

   first   that   our

   a. I wanted to buy _____ pair of shoes.

   b. We need to pack _____ cases.

   c. It was her _____ time at gymnastics.

KEY WORDS
determiners

21

Sentence types: statements and questions

↻ Recap

There are four types of **sentence**: **statements**, **questions**, **exclamations** and **commands**.

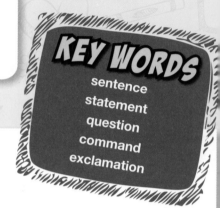

KEY WORDS
sentence
statement
question
command
exclamation

📄 Revise

All sentences start with a capital letter.

A statement: states a fact and ends with a full stop.

> London is the capital of England.   His name is Josh.
>
>
>
> Both state a fact and end with a full stop = **statements**.

A question: asks a question and ends with a question mark.

> Who is going to the party?   What are you doing?
>
>
>
> Both ask a question and end with a question mark = **questions**.

✔ Skills Check

1. Draw lines to match the sentence to the type of sentence.

Where is the nearest petrol station?   **Statement**

I wonder where I will find a petrol station.   **Question**

2. Write a question starting with the word below.

Who _____

3. Choose the best word to start each question.

When   What   Which

a. _____ time do we start school?

b. _____ is the best way to the beach?

c. _____ are you going to Scotland?

Tips 💡

Questions often start with a question word:

who   what

where   why

which   when

They all start with **wh**!

Sentence types: exclamations and commands

📋 Revise

A command: tells someone to do something and can end with an exclamation mark. It is sometimes called an imperative sentence.

> Get off the grass! Tidy your bedroom!

Both are forceful **commands** and need an exclamation mark

> Please get off the grass. ⬅ This is not forceful. It is just a polite request. An exclamation mark is not needed.

An exclamation: expresses excitement, emotion or surprise and ends with an exclamation mark.

> How fantastic! What a fierce dog!

Expresses relief or pleasure.   Expresses fear or surprise.
Both are **exclamations** and end with an exclamation mark.

> Try saying a sentence. Think about what type of sentence it is. Are you asking a question? Do you need to sound forceful or surprised?

✔ Skills Check

1. Put a tick in the correct column to show the sentence type.

Sentence	Statement	Question	Command	Exclamation
Why is the dog barking				
What a beautiful baby				
Line up, quietly				
The chocolate ice-cream was delicious				

2. Insert the correct punctuation in each sentence.

> .   ?   !

a. It was a very exciting game_____

b. You had an exciting time at Amelia's, didn't you_____

c. Make it more exciting_____

d. How exciting_____

Apostrophes: contraction

↺ Recap

What is an apostrophe for contraction?

An **apostrophe** for **contraction** is a punctuation mark used to show where letters have been missed out when two words are joined.

KEY WORDS
apostrophes
contraction

📄 Revise

We use the apostrophe to show where letters have been missed out.

he is = he's	he would = he'd
missing letter – **i**	missing letters – **woul**

they are = they're	is not = isn't
missing letter – **a**	missing letter – **o**

The apostrophe must replace the missing letter or letters in the same place.

💡 Tips

Here are some common contractions:

you are	→	you're
did not	→	didn't
was not	→	wasn't
could not	→	couldn't
I will	→	I'll
we will	→	we'll
cannot	→	can't
I have	→	I've

Exception to the rule: **will not → won't**

We often join two words together when speaking or writing informally. Try to work out what the original two words were. Which letters have been missed out? Where should the apostrophe go?

✔ Skills Check

1. Underline the contraction in each pair which has the apostrophe in the correct place.

   a. w'ed   we'd

   b. wouldn't   would'nt

   c. theres'   there's

2. Write each contraction in full on the line below.

   a. The **weather's** cold tonight.

   _____

   b. It's a long time before **they'll** arrive.

   _____ _____

   c. I **should've** finished it.

   _____

24

Apostrophes: possession

↺ Recap

What is an apostrophe for possession?

An apostrophe and the letter **s** are often used to show **possession**; to show when an object belongs to someone or something.

🗒 Revise

To use an apostrophe to show possession you need to know if the possessor of the object is **singular** or **plural**. This will help you decide where to put the apostrophe.

KEY WORDS

possession
plural
singular

Single possessor

the girl's bike

↑

one girl: apostrophe + s

the dog's waggy tail

↑

one dog: apostrophe + s

Plural possessors

the girls' bikes

↑

several girls: s + apostrophe

the dogs' waggy tails

↑

several dogs: s + apostrophe

Check how many possessors there are.

One possessor = apostrophe + s
Several possessors = s + apostrophe

Watch out for apostrophes with irregular plurals: children's sheep's

✔ Skills Check

1. Insert apostrophes in the correct places to show possession.

a. Pippis food bowl was empty.

b. The childrens outing was very successful.

c. The swans care of their cygnets was very touching.

2. Change the underlined words to plurals and insert apostrophes in the correct place. Write the new sentence.

The <u>fairy's dress</u> shimmered in the <u>candle's</u> glow.

_____

_____

💡 Tips

Before adding an apostrophe, be sure that you need to show possession.

The girls went on a long journey.
↑
Several girls – no possession.

The journey belongs to the girls – possession.
↓
The girls' long journey gave them a chance to chat.

Commas to clarify meaning

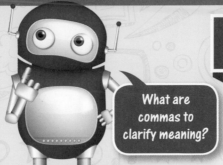

↻ Recap

Commas are placed in sentences to help us understand the meaning. Using commas within a sentence, can help make the meaning clearer and avoid ambiguity.

🗐 Revise

Sometimes the meaning isn't clear without commas.
In the following sentences the words are the same but the comma makes the meaning different:

"Can we go to see Gran?"	Someone is asking if we can go to see Gran.
"Can we go to see, Gran?"	Gran is being asked if we can go to see something.

The comma alters the meaning.
In the next two sentences, the comma alters the meaning again in the same way.

"My mother says Shona is beautiful."	My mother is saying that Shona is beautiful.
"My mother, says Shona, is beautiful."	Shona is saying that my mother is beautiful.

✔ Skills Check

1. **Explain the meaning of these sentences.**

   a. "Tell your cousin Alex."

   _____

   b. "Shall we eat Donna?"

   _____

2. **Place commas in each sentence to make the meaning clear.**

   a. "Tell your cousin Alex."

   _____

   b. "Shall we eat Donna?"

   _____

Commas after fronted adverbials

↻ Recap

What are commas after fronted adverbials?

A **fronted adverbial** is an adverb or an adverbial phrase, which is at the beginning of a sentence.
A fronted adverbial is always followed by a comma.

📄 Revise

After the monsoon, the sun dried up the ground.

↗ fronted adverbial   ↖ comma

During winter, roads are often blocked by snow.

↗ fronted adverbial   ↖ comma

✔ Skills Check

1. Place commas in the correct places in these sentences.

    a. At the end of the street there is a sweet shop.

    b. Tomorrow night there will be a full moon.

    c. Poorly cooked the food was inedible.

KEY WORDS
fronted adverbials

2. Write your own fronted adverbials, with the correct punctuation, at the start of these sentences.

    a. _____ you'll find the treasure.

    b. _____ we will go on holiday.

    c. _____ the tent blew away.

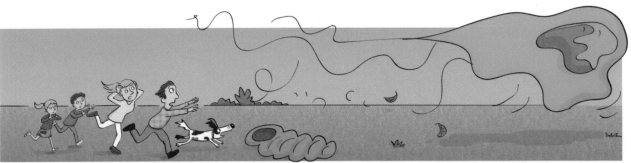

Inverted commas

↺ Recap

Inverted commas are also called 'speech marks'. They go around **direct speech** to show what is being said.

📋 Revise

Inverted commas go at the beginning and end of speech.

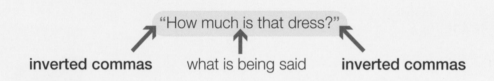

"How much is that dress?"

inverted commas   what is being said   **inverted commas**

Inverted commas *always* include one of the following punctuation marks:

| comma | full stop | question mark | exclamation mark |

The punctuation marks always come between the last word and the second set of inverted commas.

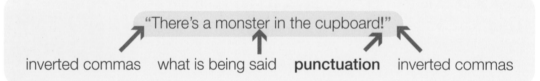

"There's a monster in the cupboard!"

inverted commas   what is being said   **punctuation**   inverted commas

A **comma** is used when the writing continues past the end of the speech.

"This is the boy," said the teacher.

A **full stop** is only used when the speech is the end of the writing. In this case, the comma moves in front of the first set of inverted commas.

The teacher said, "This is the new boy."

Question marks and **exclamation marks** are used in the same way depending upon the sentence types.

The teacher said, "Is this the new boy?"
The teacher said, "This is the new boy!"

KEY WORDS
direct speech
inverted commas

✔ Skills Check

1. Place inverted commas in the correct places in the following sentences.

   a.   Today is Monday.

   b.   How are you?

   c.   Stop!

   d.   Have you finished your work? asked the teacher.

   e.   The teacher asked, Have you finished your work?

Monday	Saturday
Tuesday	
Wednesday	Sunday
Thursday	
Friday	

2. Rewrite the following sentences with inverted commas and the correct punctuation.

   a. The teacher looked at the boy and said Well done!

   _____

   b. It will rain tomorrow said the weather forecaster.

   _____

   c. Look out shouted the driver

   _____

   d. We have some orange juice we also have some mango juice said the waiter

   _____

   _____

Tips

- Everything that is being said **and** a punctuation mark goes inside the inverted commas.
- Make sure you use the correct punctuation mark **before** the second set of inverted commas.

Remember the comma after words like said when you are using inverted commas.

Parenthesis

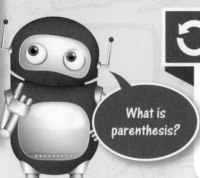

↻ Recap

What is parenthesis?

Parenthesis is the term used for a word, clause or phrase that is inserted into a sentence to provide more detail.

- Parenthesis is what is written inside **brackets**.
- **Commas** and **dashes** can do the same job as brackets.

📋 Revise

The following sentence gives a small piece of information:

My sister is getting married next week.

By adding parenthesis, more detail is given but the meaning remains the same:

My sister (who is older than me) is getting married next week.

↖ ↑ ↗
parenthesis with brackets

Commas and pairs of dashes can do the same job as brackets:

My sister, who is older than me, is getting married next week.

↖ ↑ ↗
parenthesis with commas

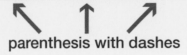

My sister – who is older than me – is getting married next week.

↖ ↑ ↗
parenthesis with dashes

Dashes tend to be used in less formal writing, such as in an email.

Remember, parenthesis is the information you add, not the punctuation around it.

✔ Skills Check

1. a. Insert the parenthesis into the following sentence, using brackets.

Toby was lost for seven days. **Parenthesis:** *a six-year-old collie dog*

_____

b. Insert the parenthesis into the correct place in the following sentence, using commas.

There are many ways to climb Mount Snowdon. **Parenthesis:** *most of them difficult*

_____

c. Insert the parenthesis into the correct place in the following sentence, using dashes.

'Grab a piece of my heart' will be number one next week. **Parenthesis:** *such a great song*

_____

d. Insert Parenthesis 1 and Parenthesis 2 into the correct places in the following sentence using dashes and commas.

My new book is going to be a best seller.

Parenthesis 1: *Wheelchair Warrior*
Parenthesis 2: *according to my publisher*

_____

_____

2. Rewrite this sentence without the parenthesis.

Our favourite place – it's so romantic – is Venice.

_____

KEY WORDS

parenthesis
brackets
dash
comma

Paragraphs

↻ Recap

What are paragraphs?

Paragraphs organise writing to make it easier to understand.

- They break text down into small sections so it is easy to read.
- They are a series of sentences about the same idea.
- We start a new paragraph for each different idea, place, time, character or event.

📄 Revise

In the following story, Jumila has been to see one of her friends.

At the end of the street, Jumila hesitated. She could see her house in the distance. She forced herself to move forwards.

↓ new paragraph because Jumila has moved to a different place ↓

When she reached the gate, Jumila stopped again. This was not going to be easy. She waited nervously for a few seconds before pushing the gate open.

new paragraph ↓   different place ↓

Jumila's father waited inside the house. He looked at his watch. What was keeping Jumila?

↑ different character   ↑ different idea

✔ Skills Check

1. a. Rewrite the following as two paragraphs.

Jumila walked slowly towards the door of the house. She did not know what would happen next. She was late and she knew it. Ten seconds later she was inside facing her father.

_____

_____

_____

b. What has changed to require a new paragraph?

_____

Headings and subheadings

↻ Recap

What are headings and subheadings?

Headings are titles for pieces of writing – they go at the start of the piece.

Subheadings are titles for sections of writing within a longer piece – they go at the start of the section.
- They make the writing easier to read by structuring it.
- They often summarise the writing.

📄 Revise

The North Pole ← **Heading** – tells us what the whole piece is about.

Who lives there? ← **Subheading** – gives a summary of this section.

Despite its ferociously cold temperatures, there is a surprising amount of life around the North Pole. Polar bears and Arctic foxes roam the land whilst in the sea there are whales and seals.

✔ Skills Check

1. Why do we use headings and subheadings?

We use headings _____

We use subheadings _____

2. Read the following article and give a heading and two subheadings.

Heading: _____

Subheading 1: _____

Round about the time your parents were born, nobody could predict the changes in communication technology. Back then, which seems like the Stone Age now, you could only write to someone or telephone them.

Subheading 2: _____

Today, you can still do things the old-fashioned way but you can also call on a mobile phone, video-conference, conference call, text, email or use social media. The future is here now!

💡 Tips

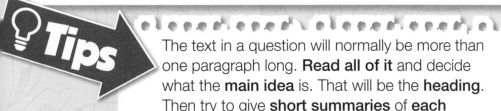

The text in a question will normally be more than one paragraph long. **Read all of it** and decide what the **main idea** is. That will be the **heading**. Then try to give **short summaries** of **each section**. These will be the **subheadings**.

Prefixes: mis or dis?

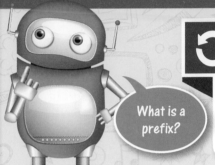

↺ Recap

What is a prefix?

A **prefix** is added to the beginning of a word to change it into another word, with a different meaning.

📄 Revise

Each prefix has a different meaning. The prefixes **mis** and **dis** both have negative meanings.

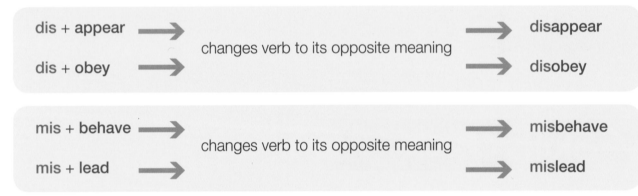

dis + appear ⟶   changes verb to its opposite meaning ⟶ disappear

dis + obey ⟶ ⟶ disobey

mis + behave ⟶   changes verb to its opposite meaning ⟶ misbehave

mis + lead ⟶ ⟶ mislead

✔ Skills Check

1. Draw lines to join the best prefix to each verb to make a new verb. One has been done for you.

Prefix	Verb	New verb
dis	spell	misspell
mis	appoint	_____
dis	treat	_____
mis	approve	_____

2. Put a circle around the word in each pair which has used the correct prefix.

a. disshapen   misshapen

b. disembark   misembark

c. dismatch   mismatch

d. disbelieve   misbelieve

KEY WORD

prefix

Prefixes: re, de, over

 ## Revise

The prefix **re** means again or back.
It changes the meaning of the verb.

recover	**re**marry	**re**write
to cover again	to marry again	to write again

The prefix **de** changes the verb to its opposite meaning.

decongestion	**de**forest	**de**fuse
to remove congestion	to remove forest	to remove tension

The prefix **over** changes the verb to mean too much.

overact	**over**eat	**over**compensate
to act too much	to eat too much	to compensate too much

✔ Skills Check

1. Choose the best prefix to make a new verb.

> re   de   over

a. spend _____

b. arrange _____

c. frost _____

2. Underline the correct word in each sentence.

a. The spy **overcoded** / **decoded** the message.

b. We **declaimed** / **reclaimed** our baggage after the flight.

c. The car **detook** / **overtook** us on the inside lane.

Suffixes: ate

What is a suffix?

↻ Recap

A **suffix** is used at the end of a word, to change it into another word and to change its meaning.

📄 Revise

The suffix **ate** can be added to nouns and adjectives to make verbs.

> elastic + **ate** = elastic**ate**
> ↗ ↗
> **noun** **verb**.

The elastic in these trousers has snapped.

I need to elastic**ate** these trousers.

Often, nouns ending **(a)tion** can have related verbs ending with the suffix **ate**.

exagger**ation** ⟶ exagger**ate**

accommod**ation** ⟶ accommod**ate**

communic**ation** ⟶ communic**ate**

Don't forget to drop the final e in a word, before adding an ending!

✔ Skills Check

1. Add 'ate' to change these nouns into verbs. Write the new verb.

   a. origin _____

   b. medic _____

   c. comment _____

KEY WORD

suffix

2. Use the 'ate' suffix to change these nouns into verbs. Write the new verb.

   a. appreciation _____

   b. domestication _____

   c. demonstration _____

Suffixes: ise, ify

📄 Revise

The suffixes **ify** and **ise** can be added to nouns and adjectives to change them into verbs.

To attach the suffix **ify**:

> pure + **ify** = purify
> ↑
> lose final **e**

> glory + **ify** - glorify
> ↑
> lose **y**

To attach the suffix **ise**:

> apology + **ise** = apolog**ise**   standard + **ise** = standard**ise**
> ↑   ↑
> lose **y**   just add suffix

✔ Skills Check

1. Underline the correct form of the word in each sentence.

   a. The butter had started to **solidise / solidify**.

   b. The children were able to **dramatise / dramify** the story of Gelert.

   c. The farmer needed to **fertilise / fertify** his crops.

2. Change these nouns into verbs by adding a suffix. Write the new verb.

   a. individual _____

   b. quantity _____

   c. acid _____

   d. terror _____

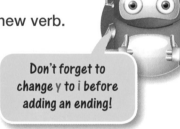

> *Don't forget to change y to i before adding an ending!*

3. Change these adjectives into verbs by adding a suffix. Write the new verb.

   a. terrible _____

   b. popular _____

   c. capital _____

> *The ise suffix is a lot more common than the ify suffix!*

Word families

A **word family** is a group of words that have a similar feature or pattern. They can often have the same **root word**, but have different beginnings or endings.

📄 Revise

Adding a prefix or suffix will change the meaning of the word and might change its function.

Start with a root word and then try adding different prefixes and suffixes.
How has the word changed?

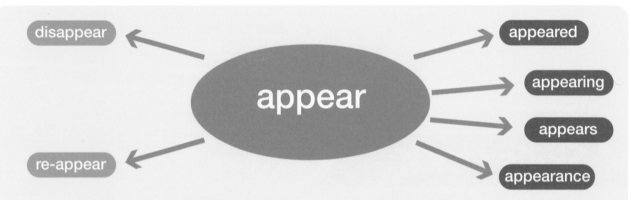

These words all have the root word **appear** but have different beginnings and endings.

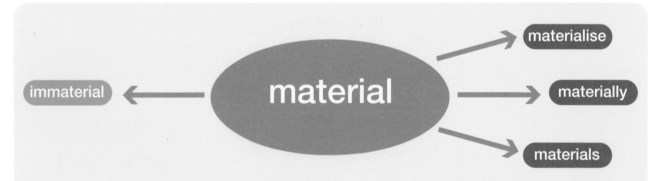

These words all have the root word **material** but have different beginnings and endings.

KEY WORDS
root word
word families

If you know a root word and can spell it, you can then make lots of other words, using prefixes and suffixes.

✔ Skills Check

1. Can you think of prefixes and suffixes to make new words?

+ prefix	root word	+ suffix
	possess	
	natural	
	remember	
	believe	

2. Colour the root word in each group.

a. accommodation   accommodating   unaccommodating   accommodate

b. insincere   sincerest   sincere   sincerely

c. dissolve   solve   solution   solving

d. continue   discontinued   continuing   continual

3. Underline the word in each group which does not belong.

a. approached   approachable   appearance   unapproachable

b. disinterested   interesting   uninteresting   imaginative

c. community   comparing   communicate   communication

d. prejudiced   prejudicial   privilege   unprejudiced

Letter strings: ough

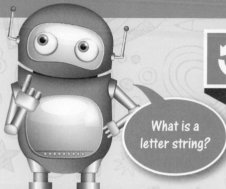

What is a letter string?

A letter string is a group of letters which make one sound, within a word.
The letters **ough** can be used to make lots of different sounds!

📄 Revise

rough ⟶ **uff** sound	cough ⟶ **off** sound
plough ⟶ **ow** sound (as in cow)	through ⟶ **oo** sound (as in moon)
dough ⟶ **oe** sound (as in toe)	ought ⟶ **or** sound (as in door)

✔ Skills Check

Say the word. What sound does it have? What letters make that sound?

1. a. Say each word and sort the sound it makes into the correct boxes.

although	bought	fought	trough	tough

nought	enough	bough	though	thought

uff sound	ow (as in cow)	oe (as in toe)	or (as in for)

b. Which word did not go in the boxes? _____

2. Write an 'ough' word to fit in each sentence.

a. I _____ I would be able to get there in time.

b. The sea was very _____.

c. We crawled _____ the tunnel.

d. The boxers _____ in the ring.

e. _____ it was very stormy, we managed to reach port.

ie or ei?

↻ Recap

What sound does *ie* make?

What sound does *ei* make?

fi**e**ld ⟶ **ee** sound (as in tree)	**ei**ght ⟶ **ay** sound (as in tray)

BUT after a **c**, **ei** makes an **ee** sound as in c**ei**ling!

📄 Revise

- In most words, **i** comes before **e**: ch**ie**f, th**ie**f, bel**ie**ve, f**ie**ld.

- After the letter **c**, **e** usually comes before **i**: re**cei**ve, de**cei**ve, con**cei**ve, per**cei**ve.

- When **ei** does not come after the letter **c**, it usually makes an **ay** sound: v**ei**n, w**ei**gh, n**ei**ghbour.

✔ Skills Check

1. Complete these words with 'ie' or 'ei'.

   a. w_____ght

   b. ___gth

   c. ach___ve

   d. n___ghbour

   e. c___ling

2. Circle the word which does not have the same vowel sound.

   a. grief   weight   shield   deceive

   b. neigh   weigh   vein   mischievous

   c. niece   relief   priest   neighbour

3. Each word has been misspelled. Write the correct spellings.

   a. acheeve _____

   b. theif   _____

   c. percieve _____

   d. wayght   _____

   e. ayght   _____

   f. retreive _____

Does it make an *ee* or an *ay* sound?

Tricky words

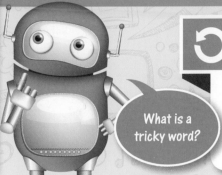

↻ Recap

What is a tricky word?

A tricky word may have:
- several **syllables**
- an unusual spelling pattern.

📋 Revise

A syllable is a beat in a word. A syllable has at least one vowel.

Let's look at a word with several syllables.

hippopotamus: 5 syllables

- You need to break the word into parts.
- Say each part of the word slowly and clearly.
- Then work out how to spell each syllable.

Ask: How do I make each sound? What choices are there?

Some words have an unusual spelling pattern ➝ y = i (as in myth)

➝ ph = f (photograph)

Here is a tricky word with several syllables and an unusual spelling pattern.

temperature: How many syllables?

Ask: **ar** or **er**?   **ch** sound, but how is it made: **ch**, **sh**, **t**, **j**?

temperature = 4 syllables

↑

Say it clearly and you can hear the **m**.

Breaking a word into syllables and then working out how to spell each part makes it easier!

✔ Skills Check

KEY WORD
syllable

1.

Colour each syllable a different colour	What is the tricky bit in this word?
build	
circle	
vehicle	
relevant	
parliament	
environment	
restaurant	

2. Work out what each tricky word is from the definition.

a. A chart showing the days and months in a year. _____

b. The group of people who decide how a country is run, headed by the prime minister.

_____

c. The ordinal number for 12. _____

d. We use it to look up the meanings and spellings of words. _____

e. An occupation or trade. _____

3. Underline the correct spelling of each word.

a. vejetable   vegetable   vejutable   vegtable

b. regular   regulur   regalur   wregular

c. seperate   separate   ceperate   separait

d. recagnize   reckognise   recognise   reconise

e. familiar   familier   familyiar   familliar

Tips

Ask an adult to read some of the tricky words in this section to you. Try to spell them. Look at the words which you got wrong. What was the tricky bit in each case? Try to memorise the words.

Double trouble

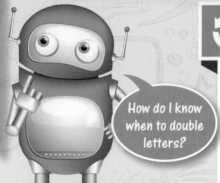

How do I know when to double letters?

↻ Recap

Some words have double letters in them. It's hard to remember when to double and when not to.

double d	double s		double p	no double r
↓	↙		↓	↙
address		BUT	appear	

📄 Revise

Let's look at words with one pair of double letters.

double m	double s	double r
↙	↘	↙
communicate	necessary	interrupt

Learn these words in groups. It helps you to remember them!

Now, we'll look at words with two pairs of double letters.

double c	double m		double s	double s
↘	↙		↘	↙
accommodate			possession	

Some words even have three pairs of double letters.

double m   double e
↘   ↙
committee
↑
double t

💡 Tips

In words of more than one syllable, a double **consonant** usually shows that the **vowel** before it stands for a short vowel sound. For example: **rattle**, **attached**, **address**.

KEY WORDS
consonant
vowel

✔ Skills Check

1. Look at the Word lists for Years 3–4 and Years 5–6 on page 76.

Sort the words with double letters into these groups.

Now colour the pairs of double letters. One has been done for you.

One pair of double letters	Two pairs of double letters	More than two pairs of double letters
	address	

2. Use words with double letters in place of the words in bold. The words do not need to have the same meaning.

a. **Parallel** lines in a rectangle are equal length. _____

b. It was **hard** to jump up that high. _____

c. We **often** go abroad for our holidays. _____

d. Uma was going to **come with** me on the train journey to London.

_____

e. It became **obvious** that they weren't going to finish on time.

_____

f. It seemed that the estate agent had **over-stated** the

good points in this house! _____

Suffixes beginning with a vowel

What is the rule for adding a suffix beginning with a vowel to a word of two syllables?

↺ Recap

- You double the end consonant if the final vowel is stressed.
- You do not double the end consonant if the final vowel is unstressed.

📄 Revise

Below are some examples for adding suffixes to words with two syllables.

for**got** + **en** = forgotten

stressed vowel sound   suffix begins with a vowel   end consonant doubled

for**get** + **ing** = forgetting

stressed vowel sound   suffix begins with a vowel   end consonant doubled

be**gin** + **er** = beginner

stressed vowel sound   suffix begins with a vowel   end consonant doubled

gar**den** + **er** = gardener

unstressed vowel sound   suffix begins with a vowel   end consonant **not** doubled

Skills Check

Is it a two-syllable word? Is the last vowel sound stressed or unstressed?

1. Add the suffix and write the new word in the third column.

Root word	Suffix	New word
begin	ing	
forbid	en	
regret	ed	
limit	ed	

Adding suffixes to words ending fer

What is the rule for adding suffixes to words ending **fer**?

↺ Recap

- You double the end consonant if the final vowel is stressed.
- You do not double the end consonant if the final vowel is unstressed.

📄 Revise

Below are some examples for adding suffixes to words ending in **fer**.

ref**er** + ed	=	refe**rr**ed
stressed vowel sound		end consonant doubled

transf**er** + ing	=	transfe**rr**ing
stressed vowel sound		end consonant doubled

BUT

ref**er** + ence	=	reference
unstressed vowel sound		end consonant **not** doubled

✔ Skills check

KEY WORDS
suffix
root word
syllable

1. **Match each root word to its correct ending.**

a. refer + ing
- refering
- referring

b. transfer + ed
- transferred
- transfered

c. refer + e
- refere
- referee

d. prefer + ence
- preferrence
- preference

e. prefer + ing
- preferring
- prefering

Suffixes: able and ably

What are the rules for using the suffixes able **or** ably?

↻ Recap

The suffixes **able** and **ably** are usually used when it is possible to hear the complete root word first.

📋 Revise

The suffixes **able** and **ably** are common.

adore + able	=	adorable
↗ lose final **e**		↖ you can hear the root word

adore + ably	=	adorably
↗ lose final **e**		↖ you can hear the root word

change + able	=	changeable
↗ need final **e** to make soft **g** sound		↖ you can hear the root word

✔ Skills Check

If able is added to words ending ce or ge, keep the final e to make a soft c and soft g sound.

1. Add the suffix 'able' to these words. Write the new word.

   a. avail   _____

   b. consider   _____

   c. notice   _____

   d. enjoy   _____

2. Add the suffix 'ably' to these words. Write the new word.

   a. rely   _____

   b. understand   _____

   c. comfort   _____

   d. consider   _____

Suffixes: ible and ibly

What are the rules for adding ible or ibly to words?

The suffixes **ible** and **ibly** are usually used when it is not possible to hear the complete root word first.

📄 Revise

The **ible** and **ibly** suffixes are less common.

terr**or** + ible	=	**terr**ible
lose final syllable		you hear only part of the root word

horr**or** + ibly	=	**horr**ibly
lose final syllable		you hear only part of the root word

However, there are exceptions!

sens**e** + ible	=	**sens**ible
lose final **e**		you can hear the root word

✔ Skills Check

You may only need part of the word.

1. Add the suffixes 'ible' and 'ibly' to these words.

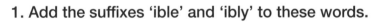

	+ ible	+ ibly
force		
incredulous		
vision		
admission		
comprehension		
response		

Silent letters

↺ Recap

Silent letters are used to write a sound – but you can't hear them when you say the word.

📄 Revise

There are lots of silent letters just waiting to catch you out!
They often pair up with another letter:

wr	has a silent w	write wrestle wrought
		you only hear the **r** sound

st	has a silent t	listen whistle thistle
		you only hear the **s** sound

kn	has a silent k	knowledge knight knee
		you only hear the **n** sound

✔ Skills Check

1. **Colour the silent letters in each word.**

   a. yacht

   b. island

   c. doubt

   d. muscle

2. **Underline the correct spelling in each sentence.**

   a. They rowed the boat towards the deserted **isle** / **ile**.

   b. I am going to **rite** / **write** a story.

   c. The **lam** / **lamb** was born just after its twin.

   d. Dad used the bread **nife** / **knife** to cut me a slice.

   e. He cut his **thumb** / **thum** on the glass.

Tips

To help you spell a word, pronounce it with the silent letter: **lis – ten**. If you can hear each letter, you will use it when writing the word.

Homophones

What is a homophone?

↺ Recap

A **homophone** is a pair of words which sound the same but are spelled differently and mean different things.

📋 Revise

There are lots of homophones.

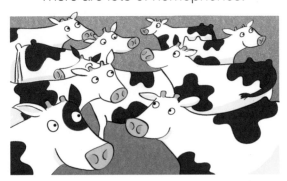

Look at the **herd** of cows.

I **heard** the birds singing.

Noun or verb?

For words ending **ce** or **se**, the type of word will determine its spelling.

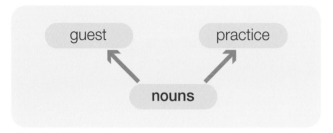

guest   practice

nouns

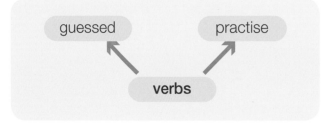

guessed   practise

verbs

KEY WORD
homophones

✔ Skills Check

1. **Choose the correct homophone in each sentence.**

   a. I **practised** / **practiced** the piano every day.

   b. The bride walked up the **isle** / **aisle**.

   c. I prepared the **guest** / **guessed** bedroom for the visitors.

   d. He walked straight **passed** / **past** me.

   e. **Their** / **They're** / **There** going on holiday next week.

Identifying main ideas

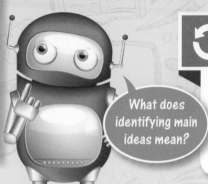

↻ Recap

What does identifying main ideas mean?

The main ideas are the important things the writer is writing about. Often there will only be one main idea in a passage.

When you identify something, you find it in a passage. To find the main ideas, decide what a passage is about overall.

📄 Revise

💡 Tips

Don't worry about each individual idea. Look for something that links them all.

In the passage below there is one main idea.

> I like riding horses. It is very exciting. I think it is great when I can see above all of the cars. Sometimes I ride very fast but never on the road.

Each of the sentences is about something different but they are all about horse riding so this is the main idea.

- Try reading the text and then thinking of a **heading** that fits it overall.
- There are sentences on riding, excitement, seeing over cars and going fast. None of these is the main idea. The link is not horses.
- Each sentence is about **riding**. So the title would be '**Horse riding**'.

✔ Skills Check

Highlight the words in each sentence that show what the sentence is about. Then try to find a link between them.

1. Read this passage and identify the main idea.

> Motor racing is full of danger. From the second the drivers get in their cars, their lives are at risk. Every corner is a hazard. Every bend is a threat to their safety. From the beginning to the end of the race, their lives are in peril.

The main idea is:

_____

_____

Summarising main ideas

What does summarising main ideas mean?

↻ Recap

Summarise means sum up. When you summarise, you say briefly what the passage is about.
A summary might be one word or a complete sentence. You need to find ideas from the whole text.

📄 Revise

You have to read the whole passage before you can summarise.
In the passage below, there are different ideas for each paragraph.

> Life was very different when I was young. We had very little money and couldn't afford to go abroad for our holidays. None of our toys were electronic and computers didn't exist.
>
> Nowadays everyone seems much better off. They all go abroad each year. Everyone has a laptop, a tablet and a games console.

← Main idea: what things were like in the past

← Main idea: what things are like now

There are sentences about the past and the present. The link between the two ideas is the difference. Put this together to summarise the main ideas of the paragraphs: the difference between the past and present.

✔ Skills Check

1. Read the passage below. Fill in the main ideas for each paragraph.

> Our cat has really annoyed my dad. He caught her scratching the wallpaper in the hall. He has only just decorated so he isn't very pleased.
>
> My dad isn't very pleased with my mother either. She laughed when she saw what the cat had done!

← Main idea _____

_____

← Main idea _____

_____

2. Sometimes, the summary is in the form of a heading or subheading. What do you think a good heading for the passage would be? Tick one.

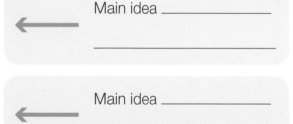

Our cat ☐   Mum ☐

Dad's decorating ☐   Dad's annoyed! ☐

Identifying key details

↻ Recap

What does identifying key details mean?

- Identify means find.
- The main ideas are the important things that the author wants the reader to know.
- The key details are what the author writes about the main ideas.

📄 Revise

Start by identifying the main idea or ideas.

> There is nothing like a day at the seaside. You can walk along the sea front; play on the beach; risk your fortune in the arcades; ride donkeys or just soak up the sun.

← Main idea: there is nothing like a day at the seaside.

Next highlight the points that tell us more about the main idea.

> **There is nothing like a day at the seaside.** You can walk along **the sea front**; play on **the beach**; risk your fortune in **the arcades**; ride **donkeys** or just **soak up the sun.**

← Each point tells us something different.

Now, use your highlighted points to give three reasons why there is nothing like a day at the seaside.

✔ Skills Check

Remember to highlight the points that tell you more about the main idea

1. Read the passage below.

> Weekends are wonderful. No school. No work. Nothing to do. Just 48 hours of selfish laziness. I usually get up late. Then I meet my mates and go into town. There's no rush and we can do what we want.

a. What is the main point?

_____

b. Give three reasons from the text to support this.

1. _____

2. _____

3. _____

Predicting what might happen

↺ Recap

What does predicting mean?

When you predict you say what you think is likely to happen. Usually you have to give reasons for your ideas. These come from clues that are written in the text. This will usually come from fiction texts.

Oh, I see. It means read the story and say what you think will happen next! This is like being a detective.

📄 Revise

Read the following passage and look for the clues to what might happen at the end of it.

> I was driving too fast. It was my own fault. I should have taken more care. When I approached the bend I started to brake. Nothing happened! The road went to the left. I went to the right. All I could see was a duck pond in front of me.

What do you think would happen next? Your answers have to be likely and realistic. A Martian spaceship could arrive and beam the driver up, but is it likely? It's probably not the right answer!

Highlight the important clues.

> I was **driving too fast**. It was my own fault. I should have taken more care. When I approached the bend I started to brake. **Nothing happened! The road went to the left. I went to the right.** All I could see was **a duck pond in front of me.**

It's likely that the car will end up in the pond. Why? The car can't stop and the pond is in front of it. What happened to the driver is anyone's guess.

✔ Skills Check

1. Read this passage. Highlight the important clues.

> I sat in the pond as the water rose around the car. Luckily, a local farmer had seen the accident and had driven across the field in his tractor. I asked him if he could help. He nodded, went back to his tractor and returned with a large piece of rope, which he waved in my direction.

a. What is likely to happen next?

Only highlight the points that give clues about what might happen. Use them to make your prediction.

_____

_____

b. Explain why you think this is likely.

_____

Themes and conventions

↺ Recap

- Themes are ideas that go throughout the text.
- Conventions are the things that help you know what type of writing it is.

This table shows you some of the themes and conventions.

Type of writing	Possible themes	Convention of this type of writing
Poetry	love, war	verses, rhyme, rhythm, figurative language
Drama	relationships	speech without inverted commas, stage directions
Fiction	myths and legends, adventure, good and evil, loss, fear, danger	heroes and heroines, villains, frightening situations, cliff-hangers, 'good' winning
Non-fiction	history, geography, celebrities, sport, gossip, cars and so on	text books, magazines/newspapers, brochures: headings, subheadings, facts, pictures, columns, bullet points

You need to be able to identify themes and conventions, and comment on them.

🗎 Revise

> That's a lot easier than it sounds! It's a bit like spotting the main ideas but I also need to be able to say how it is written.

In the passage below, the clues to the **theme** have been highlighted.

> Basitch put a few more logs under her boiling **cauldron**. She watched it bubble and hiss. Two more **toads** and the recipe would be finished. All she had to do then was to utter the **magic words** and the **spell** would be complete!

All of the highlighted words are typical of ones you would find in stories about magic. They are the **conventions**. This is different to the main idea because in this paragraph the main idea would be about making the spell, which is part of the theme of the use of magic.

The theme of the passage below is the triumph of good over evil.
The clues that identify this have been highlighted.

> Basitch hurled her spell at Srodor. He staggered backwards and **collapsed** onto the castle's wall. Basitch **cackled** loudly in **triumph**. She had **defeated the last of the knights**. Her gloating was suddenly stopped. Srodor was on his feet! He grabbed the witch by her shoulders and **heaved her over the wall**, down into the moat where a **moat monster** gratefully accepted its lunch.

To comment on the theme, explain what it is.

> **For example:** It follows the tradition that the heroes always have to seem to be beaten. Despite overwhelming odds, they always win in the end.

To comment on the conventions, show how they help the reader understand the theme.

> **For example:** The text is a fairy story. It has all of the usual elements including a wicked witch, a brave knight, a monster and a final fight.

✔ Skills Check

Highlight the clues to the theme.

1. What is the main theme in this passage?

> Sir Henry knew he would have to be brave. It was no use running away and hiding. He would have to confront the dragon; face its fire; and defeat it, even though he was very scared.

The main theme is _____.

2.

> Pauline set off across the rushing river. The water was soon knee deep and threatening to sweep her away. She forced herself across to the other side and then she set off into the woods. Her torch flickered, fluttered and went out. How would she ever find her way to the treasure now?

a. Find and copy a phrase or sentence that shows that the above passage is an adventure story.

_____

b. Explain how your phrase or sentence fits into an adventure story.

_____

c. Give two ways that the extract uses the conventions of adventure writing.

_____

_____

Explaining and justifying inferences

↺ Recap

- Inferences are assumptions that you make from clues in the text. They are the bits the writer doesn't actually tell you.
- Explain means say what you think.
- Justify means give reasons for what you think, using parts of the text to prove your points.

📄 Revise

> So this means: Read between the lines; tell us what is happening; and show us why you think that.

Explaining inferences

Some parts of the text below have been highlighted. These are the clues.

> I stopped at the kitchen door and took my muddy boots off. I didn't want to get into trouble again.

> Ask yourself, "What has happened and how do we know?"

- **What do the clues tell us?** The writer has walked into the kitchen before wearing muddy boots and this has caused trouble.

- **What do the clues not tell us?** Who the writer is; why the boots are muddy; what the trouble was.

- **What inferences can we make?** The muddy boots have dirtied the kitchen before. Someone has been annoyed by this.

Justifying inferences

Give reasons for your thoughts. To do this you need proof. This comes from the clues. In the passage above, there are two clues that you can use as evidence:

1. took my muddy boots off
2. trouble again

To justify the inference, you need to reverse the order of the clues. The most important word is **again**.

This is the key word because it tells us what has happened before and is the basis for the inference (that the writer has dirtied the kitchen before and got into trouble for it).

Now try thinking about what the clues don't tell us:

- who the writer is
- why the boots are muddy
- what the trouble was.

Can you make inferences about those? This is much more difficult as there are no correct answers.

Writing answers

Write down an inference that you can make from the passage.

> *The writer has been in trouble before for making dirty marks in the kitchen.*

Explain an inference that you can make from the passage.

> *The writer has been in trouble before for making dirty marks in the kitchen. He/she does not want that to happen again so he/she has taken the boots off.*

Find and copy two phrases from the text to support your inference.

> **1.** *took my muddy boots off*
> **2.** *trouble again*

✔ Skills Check

1. **Read the following passage and answer the questions.**

> Izzie came home from school and ran straight upstairs to her bedroom. She put her bag on her bed but did not open it. She stared at it, a worried look on her face. Finally, she opened the bag and took her end-of-term report out of it. She hid it under her pillow. She would have to give it to her mother sooner or later but not just yet.

a. How do you think Izzie is feeling?

_____

b. Find and copy a phrase that supports your thoughts.

_____

c. Do you think the end-of-term report was good or bad?

_____

d. Use evidence from the text to support your thoughts.

_____

Words in context

↻ Recap

What are words in context?

Words in context means how words are used in the passage.

🗐 Revise

When you read the passage, don't just try to work out what the word means. Try to work out what the whole sentence means.

Read the following information from a text about bears.

> Bears have to kill to eat. As a result of this, most people think of bears as being ferocious and frightening.

What does the word 'ferocious' mean in this sentence? Tick one.

violent ✔

brave ☐

strong ☐

impressive ☐

In this case, you should tick violent as it fits with frightening.

The other answers do not link as well with frightening.

✔ Skills Check

Read the following passage and answer the questions.

> The sea charged in towards the shore. I realised that the sandbank that I was standing on would soon be cut off. I tried in vain to make it back to the safety of the cliff.

1. *The sea charged in*

Which of these words has a similar meaning to 'charged' in this sentence? Tick one.

moved ☐

raced ☐

poured ☐

flowed ☐

2. *I tried in vain to make it back to the safety of the cliff*.
What does 'in vain' mean in this sentence?

_____

_____

Exploring words in context

↻ Recap

What does exploring words in context mean?

Explore means to go into the meaning of the words.

This is a bit more difficult. Now you have to look at how the words are being used as well.

📄 Revise

To explore, you have to look at a range of possible meanings of a word or phrase.

You may need to re-read the sentence or paragraph to work out what the word means.

Read this passage.

> Vietnam is a country of diverse scenery. It has high mountains, stunning beaches and magnificent forests.

Look at this question:

> *Vietnam is a country of diverse scenery.*
> What does 'diverse' mean in this sentence?

If you know what 'diverse' means, that's great. What if you don't? Read the next sentence. Look for a link to help you. **It has high mountains, stunning beaches and magnificent forests.**

The link is 'scenery'. Mountains, beaches and forests are all examples of different scenery. The scenery is 'diverse'. The scenery is *different*.

✔ Skills Check

Read this passage.

> Mauritius is over fifteen hours away by plane. This immense distance does not deter tourists. They go there anyway, despite the hardship.

1. *This immense distance does not deter tourists.*
Which of these words means the same as 'deter' in this sentence? Tick one.

help ☐

discourage ☐

disillusion ☐

exhaust ☐

Try all of the words and see which one makes most sense when you read the complete sentence.

2. Explain why you have chosen your answer.

_____

_____

Enhancing meaning: figurative language

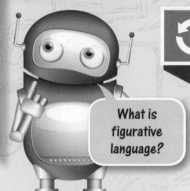

What is figurative language?

↻ Recap

Figurative language is **imagery** used by writers to create word pictures that help the readers *see* what is happening and enhances the meaning.

- Examples of this include: **analogy**, **metaphors**, **similes**, **personification**, **assonance** and **alliteration**.
- You need to write about the effect of the figurative language.

Revise

Figurative language is used a lot in poetry.

Some of the figurative language has been identified in this passage.

> The church was **as quiet as a grave**. Outside **the wind was a wild woman**, whispering **sad sorrows** across the tombstones.

Figurative language	Type of language	Explain the effect
as quiet as a grave	a **simile** – it **compares** by using **'like'** or **'as'**	You often find graves at churches. This simile links the two ideas and shows how quiet it was because graves do not make any noise.
the wind was a wild woman	a **metaphor** – it **compares more strongly** usually using **'is'** or **'was'**	This metaphor helps the reader picture the wind as a mad creature.
sad sorrows	**alliteration** – it creates an effect by repeating consonant sounds, in this case the 's'	It helps the reader hear the noise by repeating the *s* sound which makes a hissing noise like the wind.
wind, wild, woman	**alliteration**	
whispering	**personification** because the wind doesn't actually whisper	

KEY WORDS

figurative language
imagery
analogy
metaphor

simile
personification
assonance
alliteration

Always say what the effect of the figurative language has been.

✔ Skills Check

1. Read the following passage.

> The rain fell like steel spears. I was glad of it because it hid the teardrops that were swimming from my eyes before leaping and diving to the floor in pools of pain. I stumbled home like a blind man.

a. *The rain fell like steel spears.*

The sentence above contains:

Tick **one**.

a metaphor ☐

assonance ☐

onomatopoeia ☐

a simile ☐

b. Find and copy one example of alliteration from the passage.

_____

c. In the table below are examples of figurative language from the passage. In each case, state what type of figurative language is used and explain its effect.

Example	Type/explanation of figurative language
*it hid the teardrops that were **swimming** from my eyes*	
*in **pools of pain***	
*I stumbled home **like a blind man***	

How writers use language

How do writers use language?

Writers use language to have an effect on the reader through:
- vocabulary used
- use of different sentence types and links between them
- different types of text (fairy stories, newspapers, magazines, letters).

You have to write about the effect each has on the reader.

📄 Revise

Always remember to explain why and how the language that is used affects the reader.

Words

Different words show different shades of meaning – like in a thesaurus – only one will be the specific one you want. Imagine, for example, that someone has annoyed you, but how much? Did they **bother**, **upset**, **irritate**, **exasperate** or **infuriate** you? The slightly different meanings help us understand exactly what is meant.

Sentences

Different forms of sentence create a response in the reader.
- **Everybody knows that butter tastes better than margarine.** This is a **statement**. It seems to be a fact but is it? Actually, it's not a fact but it is presented as one so the effect is that the reader believes it is true.
- **Would the world be a better place if everyone tried to be kinder?** This is a **rhetorical question**. It has a clearly expected answer that the reader should agree with.
- **Dev listened carefully to see if the footsteps were still following him. Silence.** The **short sentence** has an effect because of its length. It tells us quickly what we need to know.

Text

Texts are written for different purposes. You need to be able to identify the purpose and show how the writing fits it. This one is written to persuade.

Can it get better than love?…

This includes you!

Everyone loves chocolate. Everyone loves milkshakes. Now you can have the best of both with our new Chocolate Milkshake bar. Imagine a chocolate bar that dissolves in your mouth, leaving you with that creamy, frothy, yummy milkshake taste. That's the Chocolate Milkshake bar!

…it just did.

This is what it does.

This is what it tastes like.

Read the passage below. It is from a horror story. How do we know? The words that tell you are highlighted.

> A chill wind sliced into Amy's face. The graveyard was no place to be in the dark. Around her feet the soil moved slightly. What could it be? Earth doesn't move by itself. Nothing moves in a graveyard… except ghosts! Ghosts don't exist, do they? Something pushed through the ground. What could it be? What was it? Amy looked in horror. It couldn't be. A finger!

✔ Skills Check

1. The following questions are about the Chocolate Milkshake bar extract.

a. Which word in the sentence 'Everyone loves chocolate' is meant to make the reader think that they should enjoy chocolate too?

_____

b. Why have you chosen that word?

_____

c. Imagine a chocolate bar that dissolves in your mouth, leaving you with that *creamy, frothy, yummy, milkshake taste*. What is the effect on the reader of the words in italics?

_____

_____

2. These questions are about the horror story.

Language used	Effect of language
a. *A chill wind sliced into Amy's face. The graveyard was no place to be in the dark.*	Find and copy two phrases that set the scene in these sentences. _____ _____
b. *Ghosts don't exist, do they?*	What is the effect on the reader of this question? _____ _____
c. *What could it be? What was it? Amy looked in horror. It couldn't be. A finger!*	Give two ways the writer has tried to build tension in this extract. **1.** _____ **2.** _____
d. Look at the whole passage.	How can you tell this is from a horror story? _____ _____

Features of text

↻ Recap

What are features of texts?

- Language features – the way the words are used.
- Structural features – the way the text is organised.
- Presentational features – the way the text looks.

🗐 Revise

Here are some examples of different features.

Language features	Structural features	Presentational features
• Figurative language • Short/long sentences • Variety/repetition of words • Rhetorical questions	• Table of contents • Headings and subheadings • Paragraphs or verses	• Pictures and captions • Columns and charts • Text boxes • Fonts and colour

In the following passage, a number of language, structural and presentational features have been identified for you.

heading and bold text ↘ **The New Girl**

simile · italics

All eyes turned like searchlights on the *new* girl.
She felt them burn into her. Alone. She felt so very alone.

metaphor · single-word sentence

✔ Skills Check

Do you think you're brave?

Would you go out in the dark? Would you go out in a graveyard in the dark? Would you go out in a haunted graveyard in the dark? With no moon? On your own? Alone? Yes? Are you brave? Or stupid?

1. Find and copy examples of language, structural and presentational features in the above text.

Feature	Feature name	Example
Language		
Structural		
Presentational		

Text features contributing to meaning

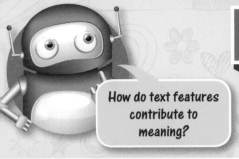

How do text features contribute to meaning?

↺ Recap

Text features are the language, structural and presentational features of texts.

You need to explain how they help the reader understand the meaning of the text.

🗎 Revise

This is the second paragraph of **Do you think you're brave?** Some features are highlighted.

subheading and bold text

repetition

Think again ↙

No one near you. No one to hear you. No one to care. Dark. So dark. Like the dark side of the moon. Are you still feeling brave? Think again.

↗ **simile**

refers back to subheading ↘

You need to be able to explain how each feature works in the passage as a whole.

Feature	What it does	Explanation
Subheading	Makes it easy to read	Breaks up the text and gives a summary of the main idea of the paragraph
Bold text	Draws attention to important text	Makes it stand out
Repetition	Builds up tension	Emphasises how alone the person is
Simile	Helps the reader imagine the scene	The dark side of the moon has no light; it is in total darkness so nothing can be seen
Ending	Refers back to beginning	Makes the reader answer the question

✔ Skills Check

Read both parts of 'Do you think you're brave?'

1. What does the use of 'you' make the reader feel?

_____

2. *Dark. So dark. Like the dark side of the moon.*

How does the writer build up tension in these sentences?

_____

Retrieving and recording information

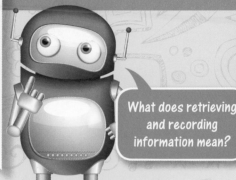

What does retrieving and recording information mean?

↻ Recap

- Retrieve means find.
- Record means write down.

Look for the first key words in the question: why, what, who, where, when or how.

📄 Revise

Read the following passage. Then look at the example questions.

The Tower of London

Sitting on the north bank of the River Thames, the Tower of London dates back almost a thousand years to William the Conqueror. At times it has been a palace, a stronghold and a prison.

For many years the Tower had a gruesome reputation. At one time, no one wanted to be 'sent to the Tower' because it meant almost certain death. Nowadays it's a tourist attraction. It's still guarded day and night because the Crown Jewels are in it, but it's not frightening any more.

Example questions

What was the reason people did not want to be 'sent to the Tower'?

is the same as

Why did people not want to be 'sent to the Tower'?

Look for the **other key words**: these tell you what to retrieve from the text. In this question they are: 'sent to the Tower'.

Scan the text above for 'sent to the Tower' and you'll find the reason – 'it meant almost certain death'.

Some questions will ask you to tick boxes. For example:

Nowadays, the Tower of London:

Tick **two**.

is on the south bank of the River Thames.	☐
has a gruesome reputation.	☐
is guarded day and night.	☑
is dangerous.	☐
is not frightening any more.	☑

Tips 💡

Look closely to find the answers!
- **Why** = find a reason
- **Who** = find a name
- **Where** = find a place
- **When** = find a time
- **How** = find an explanation
- **What** can be any of the above.

Some questions will ask you to join information together. For example:
Draw lines to link the Tower of London to its uses.

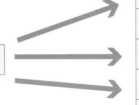

| Tower of London |

| palace |
| holiday camp |
| prison |
| tourist attraction |
| university |

✔ Skills Check

1. Read 'The Tower of London' again.

a. Where is the Tower of London?

_____

b. How long ago was the Tower of London first built?

_____

c. What kind of reputation did the Tower of London have?

_____

d. What is kept in the Tower of London nowadays? Tick **one**.

William the Conqueror ☐

Prisoners ☐

Tourists ☐

The Crown Jewels ☐

Remember to look for the key words. They tell you what to retrieve.

e. Draw lines to link the Tower of London to its history.

| Tower of London |

| has been a stronghold |
| has been frightening |
| has always had a good reputation |
| dates back to Henry VIII |
| has always been a tourist attraction |

Making comparisons

↻ Recap

Comparisons show us what is similar or different in a text.

📋 Revise

Read the following passage.

Camping
Love it or hate it, camping is big business.

What's to love?
The outdoor life. The open air. The countryside. The peace and quiet.

What's to hate?
Cold. Wet. Creepy-crawlies. Mud.

Give one reason why people should hate camping and one why people should love it.

Love it: The peace and quiet
Hate it: Mud

Read the continuation of the passage.

If you have to go camping, there are lots of choices you can make.
You could go for a cheap tent. Some even set themselves up. They are waterproof and draft-proof. You can even take a camp bed with you, so they'll be comfortable as well.

Not sure? Well, what about a moderately expensive caravan? They are easy to set up, and in the latest ones your bed's already made. You'll have running hot and cold water and even central heating!

Still not sure? You could always go for a campervan. Smart, elegant and expensive, campervans offer you all the comforts of home while on the move. No setting up. Simply arrive and start your holiday!

To compare, you have to show the similarities and the differences.

Comparison	Tent	Caravan	Campervan
Similarities – cost	Cheap	Moderate	Expensive
Similarities – set-up	Some set themselves up	Easy to set up	No setting up
Differences – comfort	Waterproof and draft-proof	Hot and cold water; heating	All the comforts of home

✔ Skills Check

1. Read the continuation of the camping passage again.

a. Give one thing that is different between caravans and campervans.

_____

b. Give one thing that is similar between caravans and campervans.

_____

2. Read the following passage.

> Today's music is rubbish: hip hop, garage, house. What does it all mean? Music was better in the 1970s than today: heavy metal, pop, glam rock. Those were the days! The artists then were memorable and their music lives on. Slade, Status Quo, David Bowie and Michael Jackson all continued to have massive careers. Today's nameless, faceless, personality-less, plastic performers will be forgotten instantly. The 1970s had real individual talents. Today's identical stars are mass produced to a formula. Of course, some things never change: record companies will always make the most money.

a. Compare the types of music available today with those of the 1970s.

_____

_____

_____

b. What differences are there between the artists of today and those of the 1970s?

_____

_____

c. What is similar between now and the 1970s?

_____

Fact and opinion

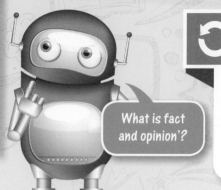

⟲ Recap

What is fact and opinion'?

- A **fact** is true and can be proved.
- An **opinion** is what someone thinks or believes. You need to be able to tell the difference between facts and opinions.

📋 Revise

Be careful! Sometimes opinions are disguised as facts.

In the passage below, there is one **fact** and one **opinion**.

> **Henry VIII**
> Without doubt, Henry VIII was the greatest king of England. The changes he made in his lifetime, **particularly to the Church,** still affect people today.

- **Fact:** The fact is that Henry's changes do still affect us today. **Can this be proved? Yes.** He was the founder of the Church of England. It still exists. Without him, it wouldn't.

- **Opinion:** 'Henry VIII was the greatest king of England.' **Can this be proved? No.** He existed and he was a king, but was he a great king or the greatest? That is a matter of opinion. It's like saying, "Which is the best football team?"

The text makes it seem as if Henry was the greatest king. How? Look at the opening phrase. 'Without doubt' disguises the opinion by making it seem like it is true without giving any evidence. It is possible to measure the tallest, widest, shortest and so on. It is not possible to measure and compare 'greatness'.

To tell if something is a fact, ask the question, 'Can it be proved?'

✔ Skills Check

Read the following passage.

> Mount Rushmore National Memorial is one of the most amazing sculptures ever made.
> Started in 1927 and finished in 1941, the memorial was carved into the granite face
> of Mount Rushmore in South Dakota. There are four huge heads of presidents of the
> United States: George Washington, Thomas Jefferson, Theodore Roosevelt and Abraham
> Lincoln. It was a hard choice! Originally, the figures were meant to be carved from the
> waist up but the project ran out of money so only the heads were completed. Such a
> sculpture will never be achieved again.

**1. Put a tick in the correct box to show whether each
of the following statements is fact or opinion.**

	Fact	Opinion
Mount Rushmore National Memorial is one of the most amazing sculptures ever made.		
The memorial was carved into the granite face of Mount Rushmore in South Dakota.		
The project ran out of money.		
Such a sculpture will never be achieved again.		

2. Find and copy three facts from the passage that are not included in the table above.

1. _____

2. _____

3. _____

3. Find and copy one other opinion.

_____

Watch out for **'weasel words'**.
They're slippery and hard to
get hold of. 'Probably' and
'possibly' are two weasel
words. They usually tell us that
something **is not a fact**.

Glossary

A

adjectives are sometimes called 'describing words' because they pick out features of nouns such as size or colour. They can be used before or after a noun, to give more detail. The red bus.

adverbs can describe the manner, time, place or cause of something. They tell you more information about the event or action.

adverbials are words or phrases that give us more information about an event or action. They tell you how, when, where or why something happened.

alliteration is the repetition of a consonant sound or letter in several words: beautiful black butterfly.

analogy is a comparison in which an idea is compared to something that is quite different. It compares the idea to something that is familiar to the reader. There are plenty more fish in the sea.

apostrophes:
- show the place of missing letters (**contraction**)
- show who or what something belongs to (**possession**).

assonance is the repetition of a vowel sound in several words: aggressive angry alligator.

B

brackets show parenthesis. They are placed around extra information in a sentence. Alex (who had got up late) ran all the way to school.

C

clauses are groups of words that must contain a subject and a verb. Clauses can sometimes be complete sentences.
- **main clause:** contains a subject and verb and makes sense on its own.
- **subordinate clause:** needs the rest of the sentence to make sense. A subordinate clause includes a conjunction to link it to the main clause.
- **relative clause:** is a type of subordinate clause that changes a noun. It uses relative pronouns such as who, which or that to refer back to that noun.

command tells someone to do something and ends with an exclamation mark or a full stop.

commas have different uses including:
- to separate items in a list
- to separate a fronted adverbial from the rest of the sentence
- to clarify meaning
- to show parenthesis.

common noun names something in general.

conjunctions

conjunctions link two words, phrases or clauses together. There are two main types of conjunction:
- **co-ordinating conjunctions** (and, but) link two equal clauses together.
- **subordinating conjunctions** (when, because) link a subordinate clause to a main clause.

consonants are most of the letters of the alphabet except the vowel letters a, e, i, o, u

contraction a shortened word where an apostrophe shows the place of missing letters.

co-ordinating conjunctions (and, but) link two equal clauses together.

D

dashes in pairs show parenthesis.

determiners go before a noun (or noun phrase) and show which noun you are talking about.

direct speech is what is actually spoken by someone. The actual words spoken will be enclosed in **inverted commas**: "Please can I have a drink?"

E

exclamation expresses excitement, emotion or surprise and ends with an exclamation mark.

F

figurative language uses words and ideas to create a mental image. Imagery, metaphors, similes and personification are all types of figurative language.

fronted adverbials are at the start of a sentence. They are usually followed by a comma.

future time is shown in a number of different ways. These all involve the use of a present tense verb.

H

homophones are words that sound the same but are spelled differently and mean different things.

I

imagery uses words that create a picture of ideas in our minds.

inverted commas (also known as speech marks) are punctuation that enclose direct speech: "Please can I have a drink?"

M

main clause: contains a subject and verb and makes sense on its own

metaphors describe something as being something else, even though it is <u>not</u> actually that. The moon was a ghostly galleon.

modal verbs tell us how likely it is that something will happen.

N

nouns are sometimes called 'naming words' because they name people, places and things.
- **proper noun** (Ivan, Wednesday) names something specifically and starts with a capital letter.
- **common noun** (boy, man) names something in general.

noun phrases are phrases with nouns as their main word and may contain adjectives or prepositions: enormous grey elephant/in the garden.

P

parenthesis is a word, clause or phrase inserted into a sentence to add more detail.

past tense describes past events. Most verbs take the suffix ed to form their past tense.

perfect form of a verb usually talks about a past event and uses the verb have + another verb.
- **past perfect**: He had gone to lunch.
- **present perfect**: He has gone to lunch.

personal pronouns replace people or things.

personification is when human qualities are given to an animal, object or thing.

plural means 'more than one'.

possession a word that shows who or what something belongs to using an apostrophe.

possessive pronouns are used to show who something belongs to.

prefix is is a set of letters added to the beginning of a word in order to turn it into another word.

prepositions link nouns (or pronouns or noun phrases) to other words in the sentence. Prepositions usually tell you about place, direction or time.

present tense describes actions happening now.

progressive or 'continuous' form of a verb describes events in progress. We are singing.

pronouns are short words used to replace nouns (or noun phrases) so that the noun does not need to be repeated.
- **personal pronouns** replace people or things.
- **possessive pronouns** are used to show who something belongs to.
- **relative pronouns** introduce a relative clause and are used to start a description about a noun.

proper noun (Ivan, Wednesday) names something specifically and starts with a capital letter.

Q

question asks a question, ends with a question mark.

R

relative clause is a type of subordinate clause that changes a noun. It uses relative pronouns such as who, which or that to refer back to that noun.

relative pronouns introduce a relative clause and are used to start a description about a noun.

root word is a word to which new words can be made by adding prefixes and suffixes: happy – unhappy – happiness.

S

sentence is a group of words which have a subject and verb and make sense. There are different types of sentence:
- **statement** is a fact which ends with a full stop.
- **question** asks a question and ends with a question mark.
- **command** tells someone to do something and ends with an exclamation mark or a full stop.
- **exclamation** expresses excitement, emotion or surprise and ends with an exclamation mark.

similes use words such as 'like' or 'as' to make a direct comparison.

singular means 'only one'.

statement is a fact which ends with a full stop.

subordinate clause needs the rest of the sentence to make sense. A subordinate clause includes a conjunction to link it to the main clause.

subordinating conjunctions (when, because) link a subordinate clause to a main clause.

suffix is a word ending or a set of letters added to the end of a word to turn it into another word.

syllable sounds like a beat in a word. Longer words have more than one syllable.

T

tense is **present** or **past** tense and normally shows differences of time.

V

verbs are doing or being words. They describe what is happening in a sentence. Verbs come in different tenses.

vowel sounds are made with the letters a, e, i, o, u. Y can also represent a vowel sound.

W

word families are groups of words that are linked to each other by letter pattern or meaning.

Word lists These are the words you need to learn to spell.

Years 3–4

accident	certain	famous	island	peculiar	sentence
accidentally	circle	favourite	knowledge	perhaps	separate
actual	complete	February	learn	popular	special
actually	consider	forward/	length	position	straight
address	continue	forwards	library	possess	strange
answer	decide	fruit	material	possession	strength
appear	describe	grammar	medicine	possible	suppose
arrive	different	group	mention	potatoes	surprise
believe	difficult	guard	minute	pressure	therefore
bicycle	disappear	guide	natural	probably	though/
breath	early	heard	naughty	promise	though
breathe	earth	heart	notice	purpose	thought
build	eight/eighth	height	occasion	quarter	through
busy/business	enough	history	occasionally	question	various
calendar	exercise	imagine	often	recent	weight
caught	experience	important	opposite	regular	woman/
centre	experiment	increase	ordinary	reign	women
century	extreme	interest	particular	remember	

Years 5–6

accommodate	communicate	equip	immediately	physical	sincerely
accompany	community	equipment	individual	prejudice	soldier
according	competition	equipped	interfere	privilege	stomach
achieve	conscience	especially	interrupt	profession	sufficient
aggressive	conscious	exaggerate	language	programme	suggest
amateur	controversy	excellent	leisure	pronunciation	symbol
ancient	convenience	existence	lightning	queue	system
apparent	correspond	explanation	marvellous	recognise	temperature
appreciate	criticise	familiar	mischievous	recommend	thorough
attached	curiosity	foreign	muscle	relevant	twelfth
available	definite	forty	necessary	restaurant	variety
average	desperate	frequently	neighbour	rhyme	vegetable
awkward	determined	government	nuisance	rhythm	vehicle
bargain	develop	guarantee	occupy	sacrifice	yacht
bruise	dictionary	harass	occur	secretary	
category	disastrous	hindrance	opportunity	shoulder	
cemetery	embarrass	identity	parliament	signature	
committee	environment	immediate	persuade	sincere	

Answers: Year 5

GRAMMATICAL WORDS

Page 6

1. **a.** They could hear the plane's <u>supersonic</u> engine.
   b. He filled in the <u>necessary</u> paperwork, before applying for a passport.
   c. She had a look of <u>intense</u> concentration on her face.

2. Accept any appropriate adjective which makes sense within sentence, for example:
   a. It was a **very delicious** meal.
   b. Nikita had **excellent** results in her tests.
   c. Their family had a **wonderful** holiday in Majorca.

Page 7

1. **a.** <u>Ellie</u> cautiously opened the dark <u>cupboard</u>.
   b. The American <u>group</u> finally reached the <u>top</u> of <u>Mount Everest</u>.

2. Accept any appropriate adjectives, for example:
   a. lazy warm afternoon
   b. deep cold river
   c. fierce terrifying crocodile

Page 8

1. The dog <u>was barking</u> loudly when the postman <u>brought</u> a letter.

2.

Present tense	Past tense	Present progressive
he eats	he ate	he is eating
they sleep	they slept	they are sleeping
we run	we ran	we are running

3. They **had finished** their tea when the phone rang.

Page 9

1. Accept either both verbs in the present tense or both verbs in the past tense.

2. **a.** was   **b.** are   **c.** appears

Page 10

1. **a.** **May** I go to the bathroom, please?
   b. We **could** go to the cinema this afternoon.
   c. They **will** be going on holiday on Saturday.

2.

Sentence	Modal verb of possibility	Modal verb of certainty
Sunita <u>should</u> tidy her bedroom.	✓	
Sunita <u>must</u> tidy her bedroom.		✓
Sunita <u>might</u> tidy her bedroom.	✓	
Sunita <u>can</u> tidy her bedroom.		✓

Page 11

1. **a.** The waves lapped <u>gently</u> around her feet.
   b. The music blared <u>deafeningly</u> from the large speakers.
   c. <u>Aggressively</u>, the dog guarded his territory.

2. Accept any appropriate adverb, for example:
   a. The snow fell **softly** during the afternoon.
   b. The sleeping baby snuffled **quietly**.
   c. The footballer **aggressively** tackled the opposing team.

Page 12

1. **a.** (During the morning) she received a telephone call.
   b. There was a fire alarm (in the shopping centre.)
   c. The cat curled up (very gracefully.)

Page 2

2.

Sentence	Adverbial of time	Adverbial of place	Adverbial of manner
Thomas played the piano really beautifully.			✓
This afternoon we will go to the park.	✓		
The traffic flowed over the bridge.		✓	

Page 13

1. **a.** Opposite sides of a rectangle are **obviously** equal lengths.
   b. **Maybe** the water will be warm enough to swim in.
   c. There is **probably** enough petrol in the car.

2. Accept any sentence using an adverb of possibility, appropriately, for example:
   We will definitely see you next week.

Page 14

1. <u>During the winter</u>, the geese arrived on the coastal marshes.

2. Accept any sentence with a fronted adverbial, which makes sense, for example: Last night, the winds blew the trees down.

Page 15

1. **a.** Although they read all the information, <u>the committee decided to close all the libraries</u>.
   b. <u>There was a flood warning</u> because it had rained a lot.
   c. After eating the meal, <u>James was full!</u>

2. **a.** The dragon roared <u>as he blew flames from his mouth</u>.
   b. <u>Despite reducing the price</u>, the house didn't sell.
   c. School had a cake sale <u>that did very well</u>.

Page 16

1. **a.** We could have a barbecue **or** we could eat inside
   b. The carpet is dirty **but** we can clean it.
   c. I am playing netball **and** I want to be on the team.

2. Accept any appropriate ending, which is also a subordinate clause, for example:
   a. They went to town so **they could buy some shoes**.
   b. She stroked the goat yet **she was still scared of it**.
   c. I love watching the swans for **they are so graceful**.

Page 17

1. **a.** I wanted to go camping **if** it was sunny.
   b. I ran downstairs **because** the doorbell rang.
   c. The door creaked open, **then** a hand appeared.

2.

Sentence	Co-ordinating conjunction	Subordinating conjunction
I met a school friend **when** I was leaving the library.		✓
We went bowling **and** we went for a pizza.	✓	
You can eat some cake **if** you are hungry.		✓
Would you like to play this game **or** play your new game?	✓	

1 a. The weather forecast, <u>that we were listening to</u>, told us there would be snow.
   b. The man, <u>whose window it was</u>, said it would need to be repaired.
   c. The pitch, <u>where the game was to be played</u>, was waterlogged.

2 The sofa

Page 19

1 The hotel

2 a. Oscar played with **his** toy engine.
   b. I couldn't wait to open **my** presents.
   c. The children enjoyed **their** swim.

Page 20

1 a. The marathon runner was <u>under</u> a lot of pressure to finish.
   b. We had to queue <u>outside</u> the theatre to get tickets.
   c. Aisha was <u>between</u> Orla and Gita.

2 Accept any sentence using 'beneath' appropriately, for example: The kitten was hiding beneath the bedclothes.

Page 21

1 a. <u>An</u> icy wind blew and <u>many</u> people were hurrying back to <u>their</u> homes.
   b. <u>Our</u> accommodation was <u>a</u> disappointment and we telephoned <u>its</u> owner.
   c. Jane arranged <u>lots of</u> tables around <u>the</u> garden and waited for <u>her</u> guests to arrive.

2 a. I wanted to buy **that** pair of shoes.
   b. We need to pack **our** cases.
   c. It was her **first** time at gymnastics.

PUNCTUATION

Page 22

1 Where is the nearest petrol station? → Statement
   I wonder where I will find a petrol station. → Question

2 Accept any appropriate question starting with 'Who' and ending in a question mark, for example: Who is going to play football today?

3 a. **What** time do we start school?
   b. **Which** is the best way to the beach?
   c. **When** are you going to Scotland?

Page 23

1

Sentence	Statement	Question	Command	Exclamation
Why is the dog barking		✓		
What a beautiful baby				✓
Line up, quietly			✓	
The chocolate ice-cream was delicious	✓			

2 a. It was a very exciting game**.**
   b. You had an exciting time at Amelia's, didn't you**?**
   c. Make it more exciting**!**
   d. How exciting**!**

Page 24

1 a. <u>we'd</u>   b. <u>wouldn't</u>   c. <u>there's</u>

2 a. weather is   b. It is, they will   c. should have

Page 25

1 a. Pippi**'**s food bowl was empty.
   b. The children**'**s outing was very successful.
   c. The swans**'** care of their cygnets was very touching.

2 The <u>fairies' dresses</u> shimmered in the <u>candles'</u> glow.

Page 26

1 a. Someone is being told to tell their cousin called Alex.
   b. Someone is being asked if they want to eat Donna!

2 a. "Tell your cousin, Alex."
   b. "Shall we eat, Donna?"

Page 27

1 a. At the end of the street**,** there is a sweet shop.
   b. Tomorrow night**,** there will be a full moon.
   c. Poorly cooked**,** the food was inedible.

2 Accept any appropriate answer containing a fronted adverbial. For example:
   a. Under the tree, you'll find the treasure.
   b. In the summer, we will go on holiday.
   c. During the storm, the tent blew away.

Page 29

1 a. "Today is Monday."
   b. "How are you?"
   c. "Stop!"
   d. "Have you finished your work?" asked the teacher.
   e. The teacher asked, "Have you finished your work?"

2 a. The teacher looked at the boy and said, "Well done!"
   b. "It will rain tomorrow," said the weather forecaster.
   c. "Look out!" shouted the driver.
   d. "We have some orange juice. We also have some mango juice," said the waiter.

Page 31

1 a. Toby **(a six-year-old collie dog)** was lost for seven days.
   b. There are many ways, **most of them difficult,** to climb Mount Snowdon.
   c. 'Grab a piece of my heart' – **such a great song** – will be number one next week.
   d. My new book – **Wheelchair Warrior** – is, **according to my publisher,** going to be a best seller. Accept also: My new book, **Wheelchair Warrior**, is – **according to my publisher** – going to be a best seller.

2 Our favourite place is Venice.

Page 32

1 a. Jumila walked slowly towards the door of the house. She did not know what would happen next. She was late and she knew it.
   Ten seconds later she was inside facing her father.
   b. There is a different place. She is now inside the house.

Page 33

1 We use headings as titles for pieces of writing.
   We use subheadings as titles for sections of writing within a longer piece to make information easier to find.

2 Heading: Any appropriate answer that is a summary of the entire passage. For example: Communication Technology
   Subheading 1: Any appropriate answer that is a summary of the paragraph. For example: As it was then
   Subheading 2: Any appropriate answer that is a summary of the paragraph. For example: How it is now

VOCABULARY

Page 34

1

Prefix	Verb	New verb
dis	spell	misspell
mis	appoint	disappoint
dis	treat	mistreat
mis	approve	disapprove

2 a. misshapen   b. disembark   c. mismatch   d. disbelieve

Page 35

1 a. overspend   b. rearrange   c. defrost

2 a. The spy <u>decoded</u> the message.
   b. We <u>reclaimed</u> our baggage after the flight.
   c. The car <u>overtook</u> us on the inside lane.

Page 36

1   **a.** originate   **b.** medicate   **c.** commentate

2   **a.** appreciate   **b.** domesticate   **c.** demonstrate

Page 37

1   **a.** The butter had started to <u>solidify</u>.
    b. The children were able to <u>dramatise</u> the story of Gelert.
    c. The farmer needed to <u>fertilise</u> his crops.

2   **a.** individualise   **b.** quantify   **c.** acidify   **d.** terrorise/terrify

3   **a.** terrify/terrorise   **b.** popularise   **c.** capitalise

Page 39

1

+ prefix	root word	+ suffix
dispossess, repossess	possess	possessed, possesses, possessing, possession
unnatural	natural	naturally, naturalise
misremember	remember	remembering, remembers, remembered, remembrance
disbelieve	believe	believes, believed, believing, believable, believably

2   **a.** accommodate   **b.** sincere   **c.** solve   **d.** continue

3   **a.** <u>appearance</u>   **b.** <u>imaginative</u>   **c.** <u>comparing</u>   **d.** <u>privilege</u>

SPELLING

Page 40

1   **a.**

uff sound	ow (as in cow)	oe (as in toe)	or (as in for)
tough enough	bough	although though	bought fought nought thought

    b. trough

2   **a.** I **thought** I would be able to get there in time.
    b. The sea was very **rough**.
    c. We crawled **through** the tunnel.
    d. The boxers **fought** in the ring.
    e. Although it was very stormy, we managed to reach port.

Page 41

1   **a.** w**ei**ght   **b.** **ei**ghth   **c.** ach**ie**ve   **d.** n**ei**ghbour   **e.** c**ei**ling

2   **a.** weight   **b.** mischievous   **c.** neighbour

3   **a.** achieve   **b.** thief   **c.** perceive   **d.** weight   **e.** eight
    f. retrieve

Page 43

1

Colour each syllable a different colour	What is the tricky bit in this word?
build	i sound: ui
circle	s sound: c at beginning
vehicle	h in the middle: difficult to hear
relevant	e or a in middle ant or ent?
parliament	ia in the middle
environment	n before ment – don't always hear it
restaurant	or sound: au in the middle ant or ent?

2   **a.** calendar   **b.** government   **c.** twelfth   **d.** dictionary
    e. business

3   **a.** vegetable   **b.** regular   **c.** separate   **d.** recognise
    e. familiar

Page 45

1

One pair of double letters		Two pairs of double letters	More than two pairs of double letters
accident	correspond	accidentally	committee
accompany	especially	accommodate	
according	exaggerate	address	
actually	excellent	aggressive	
apparent	guarantee	embarrass	
appear	harass	occasionally	
appreciate	immediately	possess	
arrive	immediate	possession	
attached	interrupt		
business	marvellous		
communicate	necessary		
community	occupy		
different	occur		
difficult	opportunity		
disappear	profession		
equipped	programme		
grammar	recommend		
occasion	sufficient		
opposite	suggest		
possible			
pressure			
suppose			

2   Suggested answers include the following:
    a. Opposite
    b. impossible
    c. occasionally
    d. accompany
    e. apparent
    f. exaggerated

Page 46

1

Root word	Suffix	New word
begin	ing	beginning
forbid	en	forbidden
regret	ed	regretted
limit	ed	limited

Page 47

1   **a.** referring   **b.** transferred   **c.** referee   **d.** preference
    e. preferring

Page 48

1   **a.** available   **b.** considerable   **c.** noticeable   **d.** enjoyable

2   **a.** reliably   **b.** understandably   **c.** comfortably
    d. considerably

Page 49

1

	+ ible	+ ibly
force	forcible	forcibly
incredulous	incredible	incredibly
vision	visible	visibly
admission	admissible	admissibly
comprehension	comprehensible	comprehensibly
response	responsible	responsibly

Page 50

1   **a.** yacht   **b.** island   **c.** doubt   **d.** muscle

2   **a.** They rowed the boat towards the deserted <u>isle</u>.
    b. I am going to <u>write</u> a story.
    c. The <u>lamb</u> was born just after its twin.
    d. Dad used the bread <u>knife</u> to cut me a slice.
    e. He cut his <u>thumb</u> on the glass.

Page 51

1   **a.** I **practised** the piano every day.
    b. The bride walked up the **aisle**.
    c. I prepared the **guest** bedroom for the visitors.
    d. He walked straight **past** me.
    e. They're going on holiday next week.

READING

Page 52

I   The main idea is: motor racing is dangerous.

Page 53

I   Dad is not happy with the cat because she has damaged the wallpaper.
Dad is not happy with Mum because she has laughed at the cat's damage.

2   The paragraphs are about Dad getting annoyed so the best answer would be 'Dad's annoyed!'

Page 54

I   **a.** Weekends are wonderful.
b. Any three from the following: no school; no work; nothing to do; 48 hours of selfish laziness; no rush; do what we want.

Page 55

I   **a.** The farmer will use the tractor and the rope to try to pull the car out.
b. The farmer has brought the rope from the tractor.

Page 57

I   The main theme is: bravery/courage.

2   **a.** Possible answers: Pauline set off across the rushing river; threatening to sweep her away; Her torch flickered, fluttered and went out; How would she ever find her way to the treasure now?
b. Possible answers: it creates excitement, it adds drama/ excitement to the story, it creates a cliffhanger.
c. The story puts the heroine in a dangerous position and ends with a cliffhanger.

Page 59

I   **a.** Accept feelings such as worried.
b. a worried look on her face.
c. Bad.
d. Accept 'She hid it', or 'She would have to give it to her mother sooner or later but not just yet'.

Page 60

I   raced

2   Accept without success, or similar.

Page 61

I   discourage

2   The distance should put people off going.

Page 63

I   **a.** a simile **b.** steel spears or pools of pain
c.

Example	Type/explanation of figurative language
it hid the teardrops that were swimming from my eyes	This is personification showing how the teardrops moved.
in pools of pain	This is a metaphor showing shape and emotion to describe the size of the pain.
I stumbled home like a blind man	This is a simile showing how difficult it was to see the way.

Page 65

I   **a.** Everyone.
b. Everyone does so I should as well.
c. They make the reader imagine the taste.

2   **a.** chill wind; the graveyard was no place to be in the dark.
b. Makes the reader wonder if they do.
c. Short sentences; asks questions.
d. cold, graveyard, dark, girl alone, strange events.

Page 66

I

Feature	Feature name	Example
Language	Short sentence Repetition of words	Yes? Would you go out
Structural	Heading	Do you think you're brave?
Presentational	Bold	Heading

Page 67

I   As if the writer is talking directly to them.

2   Repeating the word 'dark' increases and emphasises the level of darkness, taking it to the darkest thing imaginable.

Page 69

I   **a.** On the north bank of the Thames.
b. Almost a thousand years ago.
c. Gruesome.
d. The Crown Jewels.
e. Has been a stronghold, has been frightening.

Page 71

I   **a.** Anything relating to comfort.
b. Anything relating to cost or set-up.

2   **a.** Today: hip hop, garage, house
1970s: heavy metal, pop, glam rock
b. Today: Performers are nameless, faceless, personality-less, plastic performers who will be forgotten instantly.
1970s: Real talents. Artists were more memorable. Their music lives on.
c. Record companies will always make the most money.

Page 73

I

	Fact	Opinion
Mount Rushmore National Memorial is one of the most amazing sculptures ever made.		✓
The memorial was carved into the granite face of Mount Rushmore in South Dakota.	✓	
The project ran out of money.	✓	
Such a sculpture will never be achieved again.		✓

2   Any three from the following: Started in 1927, finished in 1941; Four presidents' heads: Washington, Jefferson, Roosevelt and Lincoln; Originally meant to be carved from the waist up.

3   It was a hard choice!